Cambridge Elements

Elements in Critical Discourse Studies
edited by
Gavin Brookes
Lancaster University
Veronika Koller
Lancaster University

DISCOURSE AND IDEOLOGIES OF THE RADICAL RIGHT

Teun A. van Dijk
Centre of Discourse Studies, Barcelona

CAMBRIDGE
UNIVERSITY PRESS

CAMBRIDGE
UNIVERSITY PRESS

Shaftesbury Road, Cambridge CB2 8EA, United Kingdom

One Liberty Plaza, 20th Floor, New York, NY 10006, USA

477 Williamstown Road, Port Melbourne, VIC 3207, Australia

314–321, 3rd Floor, Plot 3, Splendor Forum, Jasola District Centre,
New Delhi – 110025, India

103 Penang Road, #05–06/07, Visioncrest Commercial, Singapore 238467

Cambridge University Press is part of Cambridge University Press & Assessment,
a department of the University of Cambridge.

We share the University's mission to contribute to society through the pursuit of
education, learning and research at the highest international levels of excellence.

www.cambridge.org
Information on this title: www.cambridge.org/9781009549936

DOI: 10.1017/9781009549929

First published 2024

A catalogue record for this publication is available from the British Library

ISBN 978-1-009-54993-6 Hardback
ISBN 978-1-009-54991-2 Paperback
ISSN 2976-5994 (online)
ISSN 2976-5986 (print)

Discourse and Ideologies of the Radical Right

Elements in Critical Discourse Studies

DOI: 10.1017/9781009549929
First published online: November 2024

Teun A. van Dijk
Centre of Discourse Studies, Barcelona

Author for correspondence: Teun A. van Dijk, vandijk@discourses.org

Abstract: There has been much scholarly attention for the radical right, especially in political science. Unfortunately, this research pays less attention to the discourse of the radical right, a topic especially studied by scholars in discourse studies. Especially lacking in this research in various disciplines is a theoretically based analysis of ideology. This Element first summarizes the author's theory of ideology and extends it with a new element needed to account for the ideological clusters of political parties. Then a systematic analysis is presented of the discourses and ideologies of radical right parties in Chile, Spain, the Netherlands, and Sweden. From a comparative perspective it is concluded that radical right discourse and ideologies adapt to the economic, cultural, sociopolitical, and historical contexts of each country.

Keywords: radical right, ideology, discourse, electoral programmes, discourse analysis

ISBNs: 9781009549936 (HB), 9781009549912 (PB), 9781009549929 (OC)
ISSNs: 2976-5994 (online), 2976-5986 (print)

Contents

1 Introduction

One of the serious social and political problems in many countries has been the increasing influence of political parties and organizations of the far right since the 1990s. This development has been discussed in a vast scholarly literature, especially in political science, and far right discourse has been analysed in various areas of discourse studies. Less explicitly studied have been the ideologies of the far right, also because no contemporary discipline has developed a detailed and explicit theory of ideology as a form of social cognition, and its relations to other cognitive structures on the one hand, and discourse and societal structures on the other hand.

1.1 Aims

Within my multidisciplinary theory of ideology (Van Dijk, 1998), the first aim of this study is to update this theory with a component accounting for the combination of various ideologies that characterize political parties on the radical right, for instance, the well-known combination of nationalism and racism in what has been called nativism. After an analysis of the polarized structures of ideologies as axiomatic forms of social cognition shared by ideological groups such as (anti)racists or (anti)feminists, ideologies are related with socially shared attitudes, such as immigration or abortion. These attitudes are defined as mental representations of the social issues of actual ideological struggle, e.g., between Liberalism and Radical Conservatism. These ideologically based sociopolitical attitudes influence the opinions and emotions of the experiences of individual members of ideological groups, as represented in their personal mental models. This complex cognitive framework is needed to account for the ideological structures of discourse and other sociopolitical practices.

The second aim of this study is to critically assess current studies of the radical right in terms of populism as a (thin) ideology and elaborating a discursive approach as a theoretical alternative proposed in other studies of populism in political science but with a more explicit theory of discourse.

Thirdly, to be able to describe and explain radical right ideologies, attitudes and discourse, we briefly summarize their political context and development, especially as a reaction to the success of the fundamental cultural changes, especially in the United States, Western Europe, and other countries.

Although the main aim of this study is to account for the ideologies and attitudes of the radical right, we will briefly also review studies of radical right discourse.

Finally, the main empirical aim of this study is a comparative analysis of the ideologies and attitudes of radical right parties in Chile, Spain, the Netherlands, and Sweden as expressed in their election programmes. It will be shown that the ideological structures of the attitudes in these countries adapt to their sociopolitical context. For instance, whereas Abortion is central in radical right discourse in Chile, it is less prominent in Spain, and marginal in the Netherlands and Sweden, whereas racist attitudes about immigration are shared by all radical right parties in Europe, but marginal in Chile. Since Vox in Spain has the most complete formulation of the cluster of radical right ideologies, we'll pay special attention to their discourse.

1.2 Terminology

Earlier I have used the general term 'far right' to refer to political parties and organizations that have been described also in terms of the 'extreme right', the 'populist right' and several other denominations, whether in scholarly discourse, or in the media. To avoid confusion, and following the scholarly literature (e.g., Mudde, 2010), and has been shown in the title of this Element, I'll use the term 'radical right' for those parties or movements that (still) operate within democratic structures such as elections, as distinguished from the extreme right.[1] Since we conceive of the radical right especially as a reaction against liberalism, we may also call it the 'reactionary' or 'illiberal right' (Orbán uses 'illiberal democracy'; see also Van Dijk, 2023d).

A vast literature on the radical right uses the terms 'populism' or 'populist' as a general characteristic of parties, movements, policies or ideas. We define 'populist' only in terms of a topos (a commonsense argument), a specific, *politically strategic multimodal structures of discourse* and interaction, semantically polarizing the (good) people vs. the (bad) elites. With others, we'll argue that populism is not an ideology (thick or thin). Because parties cannot, and should not, be characterized by their discourse structures, it does not make sense to speak of 'populist parties', nor of 'populist ideas'. Moreover, not all RR parties exhibit populist discourse structures, at least not in their official discourses such as election programmes. As is the case for underlying ideologies, such as those of nationalism or racism, radical right discourse is generally polarized (e.g., between Us vs, Them) and rhetorically hyperbolic. But it would be misplaced to talk about polarizing or hyperbolic parties. Rather, political parties should only be characterized by their

---

[1] In January 2024 there are 29,200 articles since 2010 in Google Scholar with the term 'radical right' and 39,300 with 'extreme right' in their titles, and 15,000 with 'populist right'. 'Reactionary right' is used in the titles of 2410 studies, and 'illiberal right' in 276 titles.

ideologies or attitudes or their position of the political left-right scale. Hence, radical right parties (a term describing their *political* position) may also be called racist, nationalist or neoliberal (their *ideological* position). For the same reason, frequent other denominations are inconsistent with an ideological approach, as is the case for 'authoritarian parties', because 'authoritarianism', besides a type of personality, is a form of political governance or control, and not an ideology.

The widespread terminological muddle in studies of the radical right testifies to much theoretical confusion about the various political, social, cognitive and discursive aspects of the radical right. Indeed, very few studies in political science on the radical right routinely cite, use and apply advanced studies of ideology or of discourse in other disciplines. Mudde and Rovira Kaltwasser (2018: 1686) correctly emphasize that new studies of populism should be based on the existing literature on the topic. The same is true for their and others' uses of such notions as 'ideology', 'ideas', or 'discourse' in political studies of the radical right. Indeed, complex phenomena such as the radical right should always be studied in multidisciplinary frameworks.

2 Theoretical Framework: Ideology, Discourse and the Radical Right

2.1 Theory of Ideology

There is a vast literature, especially in political science, on the radical right, focusing especially on political parties and voters. Although the ideas of these parties are often discussed, this happens less in terms of an explicit theory of ideology and other sociocognitive structures. Hence, I first need to summarize and update my theory of ideology, used to study the ideologies of the radical right, to critically evaluate ideological definitions of populism and to show how ideologies are related to the discourses of electoral programmes in Chile, Spain, the Netherlands, and Sweden.

In order to focus on the ideologies and their expression in party discourse, my multidisciplinary theory of ideology will only be briefly summarized in a few points (for detail, see Van Dijk, 1998):

Ideology as Social Cognition

- Ideologies are **cognitive systems** (represented in Long-Term Memory) socially shared by members of ideological groups.
- Ideologies are based on the socioculturally shared **knowledge** of an Epistemic Community (a racist ideology *presupposes* general knowledge of other 'races', 'ethnic groups, etc.).

- Ideologies are organized by fundamental **categories**:
  - Identity (Who are we?)
  - Action (What do we do?)
  - Goals (What do we want?)
  - Norms/Values /What is good/bad for us?)
  - Reference Groups /(Who are our Allies/Opponents?)
  - Resources (Which Resources (don't) we have?)
- The structures of ideologies are **polarized** between Us/Ingroup vs. Them/ Outgroup
- Ideologies are acquired bottom-up from, and control top-down, more **specific**, socially shared **Attitudes about sociopolitical issues** (e.g., about abortion or immigration)
- Once acquired and shared in an ideological group, ideologies and attitudes are **relatively stable** (one does not become a racist or have an attitude on immigration overnight, and ideological groups are formed during a relatively long period).
- Contrary to widespread traditional conceptions ('false consciousness'), ideologies are not only 'negative' (what Others have). So, there are both racist and antiracist ideologies, feminist and anti-feminist ones.

The Social Basis of Ideologies

- Ideologies are the basic cognition of **ideological groups**, such as (anti-) racists and feminists.
- Ideological groups use many forms of **public discourse and communication** to acquire, share and change or adapt ideologies.

Ideology and Personal Cognition

- Ideologies and their Attitudes are **shared by the individual members** of an ideological group.
- Ideologies influence the opinions and emotions of individual people associated with events and actions of personal experiences represented in subjective **mental models**.

The expression of ideologies in social practices and discourse

- Through individual mental models, ideologically based opinions may be enacted or expressed in social practices (e.g., discrimination).
- The main expression of ideologies and attitudes are **socially shared discourse** of ideological groups (e.g., parties). These are also the discourses

through which attitudes and ideologies are **acquired and changed** by the members of ideological groups.

- As is the case for all discourse, also the structures of ideological discourse are adapted to the communicative situation, as it is subjectively represented by the participants in their mental **context models** (a Facebook Post, a turn in a debate in Parliament, or an election programme are different discourse genres, with different spatiotemporal parameters, different participants, different goals, different shared knowledge, etc.).

2.1.1 Ideological Configurations

The theory of ideology summarized earlier ignores the complexity of real-life ideological manifestations such as their uses by political parties. One of the theses of the present study is that the radical right cannot be defined in terms of a single ideology. This is generally the case for (political or other) collectives defined in terms of a position on the continuous Left-Right scale. Indeed, the same is true for the Right, the Left, the Radical Left, or Conservative vs. Progressive collectives (parties, organizations, voters, etc.).

To ideologically define positions or collectives, we need to introduce notions such as 'clusters' or 'configurations' of ideologies, as is often the case for the combination of Nationalism and Racism in terms of Nativism to characterize the radical right (among many studies of Nativism, see Rooduijn, Bonikowski, & Parlevliet, 2021). It should, however, be stressed that such a cluster or configuration is not itself an ideology, but a variable ideological structure that may be different in different countries. For instance, the radical right in Spain combines Catholicism with Machista Anti-Feminism, for instance, in the debate on abortion or feminism. Thus, as we'll see in this study, for each country we need to explain radical right attitudes in terms of different ideological clusters, configurations that may historically change, and hence whether or not such a configuration can be used in attempts to persuade or manipulate the voters. There is a vast literature, especially in political science, on the influence of radical right attitudes on the voters, a topic that is beyond the scope of this study (among many studies, see, e.g., Harrison & Bruter, 2011; Koller et al., 2023; Schumacher, Rooduijn & Bakker, 2022).

2.1.2 Ideological Discourse Structures

As explained earlier, ideologies and specific attitudes influence many of the social activities of ideological group members. Through ideologically biased mental models of everyday experiences, ideologies finally also influence the structures of text and talk of individual people. *Conversely, ideologies and attitudes are generally acquired and adapted through many types of discourse.* Hence, the crucial role of discourse studies and methods in the study of ideology and political parties.

The complexity of discourse allows many types of ideological influence: the choice of a word, the syntactic structure or the intonation of a sentence, the global topics of a text or conversation, rhetorical emphasis, (in) formal style, the arguments of a debate, the way a story is told, the images or music accompanying a discourse, and so on. My work on the structures of racist discourse (e.g., Van Dijk, 1984, 1993, 1998) has shown how ingroup-outgroup polarization of ideologies also influences polarized discourse structures at all levels, according to the following general strategies of what I called an *Ideological Square:*

Emphasize OUR *good* things.
Emphasize THEIR *bad* things.
De-emphasize OUR bad things.
De-emphasize THEIR good things.

Following these strategies, radical right discourse will proudly emphasize their nationalism and patriotism, demand respect for Law and Order, and negatively represent immigrants as well as socialists, and ignore or deny their racism or machismo. These are the predicted general strategies, and actual discourse analysis will need to show how exactly this is done.

With this brief summary of a more complex theory of ideology, its relations to shared attitudes and personal mental models and its expression in social practices in general and discourse in particular, we have the basic framework for the analysis and explanation of the ideologies and discourse of the radical right.

2.2 Reactionary Ideas of the Radical Right

The causes of the emergence of RR parties and their success with the voters in different countries are complex and analysed in many studies (see, e.g., Muis & Immerzeel, 2017). As always, sociopolitical and socioeconomic causes, such as poverty and economic crises, are fundamental, but seldom sufficient conditions, as we can see with the success of RR parties in rich Northern Europe. Crucial is how the causes are interpreted, conceptualized and explained, whether by politicians or ordinary citizens, and how the interpretations of the *symbolic elites* (Van Dijk, 1993), that is, those who control public discourse, are communicated to the public at large. Hence, in this study we selectively focus on the *cultural aspects* of the emergence of radical right parties and how these formulate their ideologically based attitudes on relevant social issues, as is the case for such attitudes as those on immigration and abortion.

The general theory of ideology, summarized earlier, applied to the study of the radical right, implies that there is no unitary ideology of the radical right, but rather *strategic political positions on attitudes based on various ideologies* already extant in society, especially racism (including xenophobia, antisemitism, Islamophobia, etc.) and nationalism (together usually called 'Nativism'). These ideologically based attitudes did not develop as new and original ideas of the radical right, but in the form of a *backlash*, that is, *a reaction to the growing acceptance of ideologically based liberal attitudes that have developed in large part of the world, but especially in Europe and the United States, since the 1960s* (Norris & Inglehart, 2018).

The broader these liberal attitudes were accepted and even became dominant in some countries (or in their intellectual centres and cities, among younger generations, the better educated and among women), the members of conservative parties of the Right became more radical in the formulation and propagation of *reactionary* attitudes, and formed radical right parties, as was the case also in Chile, Spain, Sweden, and the Netherlands, and even influenced major conservative parties themselves, as is the case in the United States and the UK.

We share the hypothesis that this growing backlash spreading among (older, male, provincial, less educated, economically threatened) conservative voters, manipulated by the symbolic elites (those who have preferential access to public discourse: conservative politicians, journalists and scholars) are among the main causes of the generalized move to the Right, and hence the increased support of authoritarian radical right parties in many countries. This 'cultural' backlash is especially observable in the public discourse of RR parties but does not mean that socioeconomic and regional conditions don't play a role in the growth of RR parties, as has also been shown in historical socioeconomic research (Cagé & Piketty, 2023).

In sum: the backlash against liberal values is a reaction of those losing cultural power or respect during the increase of liberal values. Depending on each country, these reactionary attitudes are often the negative mirror image of the corresponding liberal attitudes (see Table 1).

Reactionary radical right ideas and policies, as shown in Table 1, are based on relevant fragments of existing ideologies, such as racism, nationalism, sexism, militarism, and the attitudes they dominate, e.g., on immigration, abortion, gay marriage, law and order, and language policies. We'll see next how the various

Table 1 The reactionary dimension of the radical right

Sociopolitical and cultural changes since the 1960s **Dominant values**: Equality, diversity, pluralism, solidarity, collectivism	Radical right reactions and radical conservatism **Dominant values**: Inequality, supremacy, homogeneity, individualism
NATION United Nations, Internationalism European Union Globalization Immigration Anti-colonialism Human Rights Progressive parties Politics of hope and solidarity	**NATION** Nationalism Nativism, our people first Anti-immigration Anti-internationalism, anti-UN, anti-EU Love and pride for nation: Patriotism Revisionism Neo-colonialism Conservative, populist parties Politics of paranoid fear
RACE/ETHNICITY Civil Rights Movement Black Power, Black Lives Matter/ BLM Antiracism, Critical Race Theory/ CRT Diversity Increased immigration Multiculturalism Critical history (of slavery)	**RACE/ETHNICITY** White priority/supremacy Continued racism/ethnicism Xenophobia Anti-BLM, Anti-CRT Anti-immigration Anti-multiculturalism Homogeneity Anti-Islam Revisionism
GENDER/SEXUALITY/ FAMILY Feminism(s) Abortion laws Gay marriage LGBT+ Diverse families	**GENDER/SEXUALITY/ FAMILY** Anti-feminism Anti-abortion laws and practices Against gay marriage Anti-LGBT Traditional families, family values
CULTURE Multiculturalism Multilingualism Religious diversity, agnosticism	**CULTURE** Anti-multiculturalism Our language first Our religion (Christianity) Anti-Islam

Table 1 (cont.)

STATE/POWER	STATE/POWER
Liberalism	Illiberalism, populism
Democracy	Authoritarianism
Anti-authoritarian	Law and order
No/anti death penalty	Death penalty
Anti-military	Militarism
Critical of police power abuse	Police powers
Anti-imperialism	Imperialism
Socialism	Anticommunism

attitudes on social issues are different in each country, although (anti)immigration, based on (anti)racism is very general in all European countries.

As shown in a wealth of literature, the ideologies and attitudes of the radical right, as summarized earlier, have gradually become more influential since 2000, together with the growth of radical right parties in many countries, especially in Europe (of many studies, see Rydgren, 2007). This does not mean that reactionary ideas and parties are new. Indeed, many of the fascist ideas of pre-war parties have maintained their influence in underground or marginal groups or organizations. This important historical influence will not be studied here (for the continuity of radical right discourse see, e.g., Feldman & Jackson, 2014).

2.3 Studies of Radical Right Ideologies

Although studies of the radical right parties in political science hardly provide detailed ideological analysis, let us critically summarize some of the main points of this research, often formulated in terms of 'populism'.

2.3.1 Theories of Populism

Although radical right parties are often conflated in the media and even in scholarly studies with populism, a review of the vast number of studies of populism is beyond the scope of this study, even when these studies deal with ideology (see Rovira Kaltwasser et al., 2017). Again, to abbreviate the discussion on the radical right in terms of what is called 'populist' ideology, we summarize only some major points of the debate:

Populism as Ideology

The most influential scholar of the populist radical right, Cas Mudde, since his book of 2000 has also written on ideologies (e.g., Mudde, 2014). He defines populism as a 'thin ideology', i.e., an ideology that can be associated with real ideologies such as nationalism. This 'thin' ideology is defined in terms of the polarized opposition of the (good) People and the (corrupt) elite (see also Rooduijn, 2014b).

Following most theories of ideology, also the one summarized earlier, there are no such 'thin' ideologies for the following reasons: (i) Ideologies have a more complex sociocognitive structure than the opposition between the People and the Elites. (ii) Ideologies structure complex sociocognitive attitudes (such as those of immigration and abortion). (iii) Ideologies have a social basis in terms of ideologies groups (such as feminists or antiracists) – and there is no such basis for populism as ideology (see also Aslanidis, 2016).

Moreover, depending on the political situation, the People may represent different collectives (poor people, our white people or ethnic group or Volk, social class, etc.) and the elites may be any collective with power, although in most RR discourse, it represents the current mainstream government, and hence its political enemy. Such variable structures rather point to variable political debates or policies, and not to stable ideologies, and may characterize radical parties on the Left or on the Right (Akkerman & Rooduijn, 2015). In later publications (e.g., Mudde & Rovira Kaltwasser, 2018), a more general 'ideas' paradigm is advocated, collapsing such different notions as ideologies and discourse.

Harrison and Bruter (2011), in their book, propose an 'empirical geography' of the ideology of 'extreme right' political parties in Europe. They define 'a model of the extreme right as a multi-dimensional ideology based on two strategic-discursive dimensions (negative identity and authoritarianism), and four resulting ideological pillars (xenophobic, populist, reactionary, and repressive)' (p. xiii).

Confusion to Distinguish Ideologies from Other 'Isms'

Mudde (2000) and many other scholars list as ideologies 'isms' other socio-cognitive or sociopolitical structures, such as Exclusionism (an Action of many ideologies), Revisionism and Patriotism (aspects of Nationalism), Welfare Chauvinism, and Antisemitism (aspects of Racism). Conversely, family values (e.g., on abortion) are part of Christian (Catholic or Protestant) ideology and attitudes. And Authoritarianism is not an ideology but a form of governance, based on general values such as order. In other words, in political studies on populism and the radical right, there is little coherent theory on what exactly ideologies are, who has them, what their structures are, and how they are related to attitudes, discourse and political structures such as parties. See also the many 'isms' discussed in their study of Latin America (Bar-On & Molas, 2021)

Populism as Strategic Discourse

The polarized opposition between the (Good, Noble) People and the (Bad, Corrupt) Elites, with their various identities depending on the sociopolitical context, suggests that this polarization is discursive, e.g., a common strategy of much political discourse, and even a standard argument (*topos*) of political debate. In my earlier studies of racist discourse in politics, conservative MPs in the UK already defended anti-immigration policies in terms of the wishes attributed to their constituents (see, e.g., Van Dijk, 1991, 1993). Thus, until today, in the UK, as elsewhere in Western Europe and the United States, the attributed anti-immigrant views of the 'people' are positively compared to the alleged pro-immigration views or policies of the 'elites' of the Left.

Aslanidis (2016), rejecting the 'thin ideology' thesis, proposes that such a discursive structure is a kind of frame, but he provides no analysis of the discourse structures of such frames. Discourse with such 'populist' (semantic) structures, is part of a broader 'political strategy' to seek the support of large groups of followers (Weyland, 1996). Bonikowski (2017) also criticizes the conflation of populism and ethno-nationalism or authoritarianism and proposes to carefully distinguish these notions. In his 'minimalist' approach, he defines populism as a 'form of political discourse (. . .) Rather than treating populism as a property of parties and candidates, it becomes more useful to measure it at the level of political speeches, or even speech elements'.

Jagers and Walgrave (2007) more specifically define populism as a 'political communication style', hence also as a property of discourse. However, 'style' in political studies is often used as any discourse structure to communicate the same meaning, and hence may be linguistic style, rhetoric, performance or typography.

Thus, whereas several authors define populism in terms of discourse, they generally fail to define or identify which discourse structures are involved, mostly because they fail to consult or apply contemporary discourse studies. See also Stavrakakis et al. (2017) for a discourse approach of populism.

2.3.2 Left vs. Right Populisms

Though not the topic of this study about the radical right, we briefly need to comment on the (real or alleged) populism(s) of the Left (among many studies see, e.g., Agustin, 2019; Charalambous & Ioannou, 2019; Flesher Fominaya, 2020).

If populism is defined in strategic discursive terms, it obviously may also be a property of the discourse of (radical) left parties, also aiming to persuade 'the people' to vote for them. But there is a fundamental difference between populisms of the left and the right. Whereas at the right, populist discourse manipulates citizens, or rather 'ordinary people', to vote for a party that claims to struggle for their interests, but its neoliberal ideologies and policies are not social at all. In other words, in RR party discourse, there is a discrepancy between the ideologies and populist discourse structures. Such is also the case for the actual policies when RR parties come to power.

On the left, the topos of 'people vs. elite', typical of much political discourse, is an expression of polarized (Us vs. Them) underlying (socialist) ideologies and implemented in policies that do favour 'ordinary people'. Whereas traditionally the socialist opposition was between the workers and the owners or capitalists, contemporary versions of socialism would be much broader and more flexible, both at the US and the THEM side, also depending on the sociopolitical context of the country.

Hence, depending on the various meanings of 'populism', including negative ones, *one might ask why the use of the 'people vs. elite' topos in socialist party discourse is called 'populist' in the first place, and not simply 'socialist'*. Of course, such an ideologically based (semantic) topos maybe formulated in more or less 'populist' styles. *But in that case it should rather be called 'popular'*, as is more generally the case in the sociolinguistic sense of 'popular language use' in a broader discourse analytical framework (of many studies, see Eckert & Rickford, 2001). This may include not only lexical choice or grammar, but also specific pragmatic, rhetorical, narrative and many other discursive structures that have (more) influence among 'ordinary people', and to whom such discourse is addressed by what is often called 'recipient/audience design' (Bell, 1984; for an application in politics, see Laube, 2020). Discourse analytical studies of RR parties have extensively paid attention to such specific discourse structures (among many studies, see, Angouri & Wodak, 2014; Ekman & Krzyzanowski, 2021; Ekström, Patrona & Thornborrow, 2018; Wodak, 2021; and see further).

Further detailed and systematic analysis comparing radical left and right party discourse is necessary to find out whether the differences are not just ideological (e.g., as socialist vs. neoliberal). One might hypothesize that the people vs. elites topos in left/socialist discourse takes place at several levels of discourse, and more extensively related to all societal domains, repeatedly expressing values such as those of equality, justice, and broadly including many collectives, such as women, LBGT+, immigrants, and so on. In populist discourse on the (radical) right, it would be rather a slogan to repeatedly refer to the people (or the citizens) in order to formulate, on the one hand, the many enemies of the radical right party: from the mainstream parties in politics, the unions, social movements, the EU, etc., and, on the other hand, all those excluded or ignored in society, as is the case for poor people, women, queer people, immigrants, and so on.

In sum, we assume that discourse of (radical) left discourse using the people vs. elite topos should be called *socialist (*or *social-democratic)*, whether or not it uses a 'popular' style, and not 'populist', because it is based on a socialist ideology, as is also shown in other discourse structures, especially general topics, such as forms of the distribution of wealth, exploitation, the experience of poor people, and the use of specific socialists values, such as equality (see Bastow, 2019; Wuthnow, 1989). Conversely, discourse of RR parties using the same topos is populist as a pseudo-socialist strategy, based on different ideologies, also shown in many other structures of discourse.

In sum, on the left and the right, not only the underlying ideologies would be very different, but beyond the simple 'people vs. elite' topos, there would be many detailed other ideologically differences of meaning and form. For radical right party discourse, we'll observe some of these differences in our comparative analysis next.

2.4 Discourses of the Radical Right

Within the general framework outlined above about the sociocognitive structures of ideologies, their relations to other mental structures and processes and their 'expression' in social practices such as those of text and talk, we need to specifically focus on the discourses of the radical right. *These discourses are the only data of an empirical study of ideologies as a form of social cognition.*

My thesis, applied in many earlier studies, especially on (anti) racist discourse, is that such discourse is generally polarized between US and THEM at all levels of discourse. But this thesis is very general and may apply to most ideologically based political discourse, also on the left. So, the analysis needs to be more specific.

I also argued earlier that actual ideological struggle and debate, whether of (e.g., racist) domination or (antiracist) resistance, does not usually take place at the very general and abstract level of ideologies, but rather at the level of socially shared attitudes, such as those on abortion and immigration. Hence, the more specific discourses of the radical right, as we'll see in more detail next for Chile, Spain, the Netherlands, and Sweden, will of course be about such attitudes, although with personal or contextual variations (based on individual mental models).

Such discourses – as is the case for all discourse – also depend on *context* (as subjectively defined in the *context models* of participant authors and recipients) and hence are adapted to the intended audience (Van Dijk, 2008). Some discourse genres, such as election programmes or manifestos are relatively general, abstract and hence less contextual and more directly express the dominant ideologies and attitudes of a party and its leaders (van Dijk, 2023b). This is the reason why we analyse electoral programmes of political parties in this study, rather than the personally variable discourses of social media posts that are also influenced by a large variety of personal histories and experiences (represented in personal mental models), such as losing a job or as a fight with a foreign neighbour, that could explain *why* people vote for a specific party.

Hence, the analysis of election programmes next offers quite reliable insight in the socially shared ideological attitudes of the political parties. But their semantic detail, style, rhetoric and other 'local' variation will be influenced by the strategic communicative goals of the party, the addressees, whether more or less radical or moderate, and various other contextual variables, inclusive usual conditions of politeness and deference.

This means that the discourse structures of the radical right depend on the communicative and broader sociopolitical contexts – as interpreted/construed by the authors – and the context-dependent discourse genre. Hence, more or less official, public texts such as election programmes or manifestos will have a more formal style than debates in parliament. They are much less formal in spontaneous media programmes or street discourse of politicians – which no doubt will also be more radical. The same is the case of social media posts of party members.

2.4.1 A Brief Review of Discourse Studies of the Radical Right

As is the case for general political studies of the radical right, also its discourses have frequently been studied, generally by linguists rather than by political scientists (see, e.g., Hidalgo Tenorio, Benitez-Castro & De Cesare, 2019; Kopytowska, 2017; Wodak, 2021; Wodak, KhosraviNik & Mral, 2013; Zienkowski & Breeze, 2019).

Unfortunately, there are many studies of RR discourse that do not engage in any kind of systematic discourse analysis. Some papers use traditional content analysis of populism, as is the case in the paper by Bernhard and Kriesi (2019), analysing party discourses of 11 national elections in Europe between 2012 and 2015. One of their conclusions is that radical parties (of the left and the right) use populist appeals more than mainstream parties, but that on cultural issues the radical right uses more populist appeals, whereas the radical left focuses on economic issues (see also March, 2017).

This result shows that populist appeals in general are anti-elitist because radical parties (of the left or the right) generally are not in power. As we have seen above, RR populism is reactionary because of the issues of the culture war, whereas the left represents rather an ideologically based, *popular* defence of (poor) people, and hence is socialist and not populist according to the theory defended here.

Bobba and McDonnell (2016), in their analysis of RR parties in Italy, show that when the Lega Nord and Forza Italia came to power, they do not change their populist discourse, although the 'elites' may be different. This means that in the discourse of RR parties the identity of the elites depends on the political context (for instance in Spain it is the left or the social-democratic government), whereas in political discourse of the left the elites are –by definition of the underlying socialist ideology—those who have socio-economic power and abuse of such power to exploit 'ordinary people'.

As is quite common in political science, other notions are used in the literature to refer to discourse, such as the more specific notions of 'rhetoric' or 'narrative', nor are theories and methods of discourse studies used. Instead, a more philosophical approach, such as the work of Laclau (2005), is often used without reference to theories of linguistically oriented discourse studies.

2.4.2 Studies of Discourse Structures of RR Party Discourse

Among the many studies of RR Party discourse, especially those based on Critical Discourse Studies (CDS) have made many important contributions, also because they focus on more specific properties of discourse, and not just a general polarization between the people and the elite, or between our people and immigrants.

No doubt the major publication based on sophisticated CDS analyses has been the seminal book by Ruth Wodak *The Politics of Fear* (2020), which also reviews and applies many other CDS analysis of RR discourse. Besides theoretical analyses of RR politics, the study also features many case studies, for instance of RR politicians in Austria, Hungary, Germany, the United States, Italy, Greece and other countries. Instead of a detailed review of this book, we summarize the kind of discourse structures discussed in her analysis of RR discourse of which in general she analyses the many types of 'normalization'. Wodak studies the following discourse structures and strategies in a large variety of discourse genres, such as caricatures, posters, emails, speeches of politicians, websites, symbols, Facebook posts, editorials, parliamentary debates, rap songs, TV debates, and interviews, especially of RR politicians in various countries:

- Alternative facts
- Denials of racism/antisemitism
- Caricatures

- Arrogance of ignorance
- Fallacies
- Topoi (many types of, especially of history)
- Anti-intellectualism
- Bad manners
- Scapegoating
- Calculated ambivalence
- Doublethink and doublespeak
- Coarse civility
- Conspiracy theories
- Others as parasites
- Perpetuum mobile
- Anti-genderism
- Anti-Muslim rhetoric
- Flooding metaphors
- Othering
- Appeals to feelings
- Stereotyping
- Provocation

Since most populist approaches to the study of RR parties are based on some kind of discourse analysis, many studies find variable expressions of the opposition between (good) people and (bad) elites or governments (e.g., comparing Vox in Spain and the Lega in Italy: Cervi, Tejedor, & Villar, 2023). Many of these discourse structures have been analysed in more focused studies (e.g., for conspiracy narratives have been analysed in Musolff, 2022).

Within a CDA framework, Abdeslam (2021) analysed the 'populist' discourse of the French radical right party *Rassemblement National* describing immigrants and especially Muslims (and the 'lawless' cities where they live) as illegal and criminal and as an 'Islamist' threat of ordinary French people, and their political opponents as those responsible for immigration. What are analysed are the (semantic) structures expressing a Nativist (Nationalist-Racist) ideological cluster and using the populist discourse strategy to defend (French) people and blaming the elites in power. As is usually the case in such populist discourse, the political function of such discourse is to attack the (Macron) government, and to get (more) votes from (French) people.

In a study of the discourse of Santiago Abascal, leader of RR party Vox in Spain, Barrio (2021) arrives at similar conclusions. Abascal positively represents the (good)(Spanish) people and negatively the 'elites', i.e., the (left) government and progressive media, excluding immigrants from outside and (terrorist group) ETA supporters in Basq country, and Catalan 'independentistas' from the inside. Hence, the populist strategy at the same time expresses the ideologies of nationalism ('strong Spain', centralism) and racism (against immigrants). In this case, the analysis also focuses on aggressive, chummy, and vulgar language. It should be noted, however, that populist 'anti-elitism' of Abascal and Vox is not a general criticism of the powers that be, but – as usual— a political attack on the (current, left) government, as we'll see in more detail next.

Comparing RR movements in the UK and France, Braouezec (2016) shows that despite political differences these parties share specific (semantic, thematic) patterns of discourse, such as: national heritage, a Golden Age, a violent future, criticism of immigration, Great Replacement Theory (according to which white people will be eventually replaced by non-white people because of immigration), political correctness, or 'wokeness' and multiculturalism. Although the author does not offer an ideological analysis, the topics covered are again typical of a combination of nationalist and racist ideologies.

Some more specific properties of the discourse of RR parties are analysed in the following studies: RR discourse may be less hateful, so as to avoid legal problems (see, e.g., Serafis & Boukala, 2023). For the same reason, RR party discourse, e.g., on immigration, often features denials, equivocation and doublespeak (as is the case for the BNP in the UK: Bull & Simon-Vandenbergen, 2014; Edwards, 2012; see also Engstrom & Paradis, 2015).

The polarized opposition between the people and the elites is sometimes defined as a 'frame' (Caiani & Della Porta, 2011). RR party discourse on immigration, as is the case for Vox in Spain, typically construes 'bulos' (hoaxes) and other fabricated stories to criminalize immigrants and to produce fear among the population (Camargo Fernández, 2021)

One of the strategies of RR parties is the delegitimation of Europe (as is the case for the AfD in Germany during the COVID crisis: Forchtner & Ozvatan, 2022).

One of the ways to define populism, as we have seen above, is to do so in terms of a specific communication style 'displaying proximity to the people' (as in a study of Vlaams Blok: Jagers & Walgrave, 2007) – although this would require a more specific sociolinguistic theory of style.

One typical topic of RR discourse is also the struggle between Christianity and dominant political forces (Lamour, 2022). Many studies on RR positions on immigration in Europe are Islamophobic, and represent Muslims as violent, irrational villains and Islam as a threat of which (our) people are victims (on RR parties in Austria, Germany and Italy, see Oztig, 2023; for the Netherlands, see further).

RR discourse may be metaphorically analysed as a form of 'weaponization of language' such as propaganda, disinformation, censorship, and mundane discourse (Pascale, 2019). RR discourse may feature the well-known metaphorical opposition between a strict father and a self-sacrificing mother (Rheindorf & Wodak, 2019). RR discourse is often characterized as 'debasing political rhetoric': as aggressive, impolite, rude, insulting, and uncivil, thus breaking the values and norms of 'parliamentary' discourse (of many studies, see Block, 2022; Boatright, 2019; Feldman, 2023; Macaulay, 2019; Wodak, 2021).

2.5 Election Programmes

Radical right parties practice a large number of different discourse genres (Cap & Okulska, 2013). Next we only analyse party manifestos or election programmes, with their own typical text and context structures. But of course, RR-parties and their leaders and other members also participate in parliamentary debates, produce website (and its many specific digital genres) and blogs. RR politicians give speeches and interviews and routinely engage in campaigns and conversations. RR-demonstrations carry or shout slogans, adding to the large variety of linguistic landscapes on the streets. Many of these discourse genres have been studied in various disciplines, especially in the political sciences and discourse studies.

Although this study is primarily about the ideologies and attitudes of RR parties, the empirical analyses below are based on the texts of election programmes, because we have assumed earlier that these programmes more systematically and explicitly express underlying ideologically attitudes. So, we also need to comment on discursive structures and strategies typical of the genre, or typical of RR discourse (for political studies of election programmes, see, e.g., Budge et al. 1987; there are many specific studies of election discourse – see further – but as yet there are no general studies of election programmes as a genre).

2.5.1 Communicative Context

As a genre, election programmes not only need to be defined, as is more traditionally the case, in terms of their complex discourse structures at various levels of analysis, such as their local or global meanings, but also in the pragmatic terms of the structures of the communicative situation expressed or 'indexed' by various kinds of discourse structure.

Different from sociolinguistic approaches, my theory of the communicative context (Van Dijk, 2008) claims that there can't be a direct influence of the communicative context on the structures of discourse – because they are different kinds of structure. Rather, how the communicative context influences discourse structures is *cognitively mediated* by the context models of the discourse participants: how they subjectively define that context. It is this context model that is applied in discourse production and that makes sure that the discourse is pragmatically 'appropriate' in the current communicative situation. This is also the case for the genre of election programmes. Without a detailed account of the structures of the communicative context (for theory and much detail, see Van Dijk, 2008), I'll assume here that such contexts consist of a Space, Time, Participants (and their Identity, Role, and Relations), an Action and Goals, Knowledge about the knowledge and ideology of the recipients (Common Ground).

Thus, the communicative context of the genre of an election programme is the spatiotemporal period before an election, the principals are presidents or other leaders of a political party, the addressees the public at large, the communicative act an assertion about the ideas or policies of the party – and possibly accusations against political opponents or the current government, with the Goal to get votes, and the Knowledge about the main current events and situation of the country shared by all members of the Epistemic Community, and finally the Ideologies of the party, and assumptions of the ideologies of the public.

These are the structures that will systemically influence many of the structures of the election programme, such as its style and other variable structures that depend on this kind of communicative situation. For instance, as published official discourse of a political party, it is likely that election programmes are relatively formal, and at least more formal than parliamentary debates, and especially more formal than spontaneous speeches of politicians or members of a party in one of the many genres of discourse mentioned earlier, for instance during a debate, conversation or demonstration.

Of course, the communicative situation is a specific (communicative) part of the more general *sociopolitical, cultural, and historical contexts* that systematically influence – also through a cognitive interface– the local and global meanings of the election programmes – so that, indeed, they are very different in different countries and periods.

2.5.2 The Semantics of Election Programmes

It is under the influence of the communicative and broader sociopolitical contexts that the actual 'contents' of election programmes are formulated in terms of the local meanings of words and sentences, and the global meanings of the main topics of the programme, typically organized in chapters about domains of society, such as the economy or education. As we'll see next, RR parties typically dedicate chapters to the nation, immigration, crime, and security. Given the polarization of underlying ideologies and attitudes, also the semantic and lexical structures of the election programme will be polarized between (Good) Us vs. (Bad) Them. Pragmatically, election programmes typically engage in promises.

At the local level of words and sentences, such semantic structures may be organized in terms of arguments and enhanced by rhetorical structures such as hyperboles and the ubiquitous 'numbers game'.

2.6 Conclusion of Theoretical Framework

With this summary of my updated theory of ideology, applied to RR political parties, their relations to more specific ideological attitudes, personal opinions in mental models, and finally expressed in many different structures of ideological discourse and other social practices, we now have the multidisciplinary framework to study the election programmes of the radical right in Chile, Spain, the Netherlands, and Sweden. As planned, this analysis will largely be ideological, but also some typical discourse structures of these programmes will be noticed. However, a detailed analysis of all the relevant discourse structures of these programmes would require a multilevel analysis that is beyond the scope of this study.

Since the election programmes of these countries are in Spanish, Dutch, and Swedish, a more detailed discourse analysis would be needed to account for specific expressions in these languages, for instance, in terms of a study of the 'popular' style of some of these programmes mentioned earlier, as is especially the case for Spain and the Netherlands. Also for reasons of comparison, this is also why this study focuses on ideological structures rather than on detailed discourse structures.

3 Comparative Analysis of Election Programmes in Chile, Spain, the Netherlands, and Sweden

Within the theoretical framework summarized earlier, we analyse and compare the ideological structures of recent electoral programmes in Chile, Spain, the Netherlands, and Sweden.

The choice of these countries is based on various considerations. We are interested in the influence of different national and regional contexts on the ideological clusters as they influence the attitudes and hence the policies of the electoral programmes of the Radical Right, e.g., according to the following (overlapping) parameters defining Chile, Spain, the Netherlands and Sweden:

- Countries of the Global North vs. Countries of the Global South
- European vs. Non-European countries
- Northern vs. Southern European countries
- Countries with and without a liberal/progressive consensus
- Rich vs. Poor Countries
- Protestant vs. Catholic Countries
- Countries with and without a colonial past
- Countries with and without a recent dictatorial past
- Countries with different languages

It goes without saying that to account for such differences a vast, also quantitative, research programme would be necessary to account for ideological influences of these contexts. This study, however, is qualitative and hence requires more detailed ideological analysis of electoral programmes, an approach that may serve for the elaboration of more encompassing research projects.

3.1 Chile: The Partido Republicano

The Republican Party (the *Partido Republicano*) in Chile was founded in 2019 by its radical right leader, José Antonio Kast, who earlier was a member of the UDI conservative party. In 2021 he ran for president but lost (against left-wing candidate Boric) with 44.1 per cent of the vote, showing the continued considerable force of the (radical) right in Chile after the dictatorship of Pinochet. Indeed, Kast was often accused to be a 'pinochetista' because of his connections with notorious figures of the Pinochet era or lack of explicit condemnations of the violations of Human Rights during Pinochet's dictatorship. Similarly, there are also examples of Kast's negative attitudes about LGBT+ groups.

As is the case for its leader, also the Republican Party (and its ideology) has been variously described as authoritarian, conservative, nativist, nationalist and populist by national and international media and scholars. Such descriptions only partly account for its ideologies (nationalism), but rather for ideological complexes (nativism), and types of regime (authoritarian) (for studies of the contemporary radical right in Chile, see, e.g. Bar-On & Molas, 2021; Barria Asenjo et al., 2022; Borges, 2021; Caro & Quitral Rojas, 2023; Diaz, Kaltwasser & Zanotti, 2023; Farré, 2017; González Fuentes, 2017; Sznajder, 2015).

3.1.1 The Electoral Programme of the Partido Republicao

My method of analysis is to focus first on the overall meanings or main topics (semantic macrostructures) of the foundational text of the party, namely its 'guiding principles' as presented on its website. Unfortunately, there is no space for detailed discourse analysis of this text. So, the main objective of the analysis is to infer the ideologies and attitudes. This text, in Spanish, has 2,974 words. Its initial summary is as follows:

(1) ***Our guiding principles***

Defending your life from conception to natural death

In the Republican Party we believe in God

We believe in life in Society that promotes the Family as its fundamental nucleus.

We believe in good and truth as objective realities.

We believe in the common good, defending and vindicating the concept of Homeland.

We defend the Freedom of the People and of the Intermediate Bodies.

We believe in Social Justice

We believe in a Social Market Economy

We promote Decentralisation

We believe in a Modern and Transparent State, a Quality, Reliable and Firm Institutionality.

The fact that this text fragment appears at the beginning of the 'Principles' document suggests that it may be interpreted as the dominant, overall summary of which the rest of the text elaborates the details, as is also the case for an analysis of headlines in the press. Related to the structures of the underlying ideologies, we may infer the following ideological cluster and some of its attitudes, as follows (see Table 2):

Table 2 Main ideologies and attitudes
of the Republican Party in Chile

Ideologies	Attitudes +Positive – Negative
Catholicism	-Abortion
	-Euthanasia
	+Family
Nationalism	+Homeland, +Patriotism
	-Centralization
Liberalism	+Freedom of the people
	+Social Justice
Neoliberalism	+Social Market Economy

This is merely an abstract summary (which will not be repeated for each country), so it is not yet clear what exactly its attitudes imply, as is the case for the liberal (positive) attitudes Freedom of the People and Social Justice. However, the dominant ideology and attitudes are explicitly those of Catholicism, although the actual text denies the party is a religious party. We have seen earlier that such denials as well as ambiguity are quite typical of RR discourse. Interesting is the attitude on Decentralization, which usually (as in Spain) would not be consistent with centralized nationalism.

For ideological analysis, it is crucial that the organization of a text in terms of Summaries and Tables of Content provides suggestions for the organization of ideologies and attitudes and their relevance or importance. Hence, the first and most prominent statement of the Summary ('Defending your life from conception to natural death') also reflects the prominence of anti-abortion and anti-euthanasia as major Attitudes of the Republican Party and its Catholic ideology.

Interesting is also the belief in 'good and truth as objective realities', which are (very general) values, rather than ideologies or attitudes, but no doubt included in the summary as implicitly against its opposed values. The rest of the text dedicates a whole chapter to this belief, and explains it as follows:

(2) Both concepts are rationally knowable by any person, and they are found in the notion that every human being has of that set of objective moral virtues, which respond to the natural order of things, and which can never be modified either by any political authority, or by any electoral or parliamentary majority.

Although even this fragment is still very abstract and vague, its implied opponent (parliamentary majorities) most likely refers to the international debate and laws on gender, against the assumed 'objective reality' of sex. In other words, the values mentioned here are those based on the Catholic definition (i.e., denial) of gender, and the Attitude is about so-called 'Gender Ideologies'.[2]

For ideological analysis this example shows that ideologies and attitudes cannot always be deduced from explicit formulations of official programmes but need to be inferred from implicit information and social, political, or cultural contexts. This is especially the case if the attitudes are contentious and (as in this case) contrary to general policies (of parliament) or scientific consensus (e.g., on gender). In this case, the more specific opponent of the attitude are democratic parliaments, which also means that radical right parties may be less democratic. In other words, for this party, the 'natural order of things' and 'rational knowledge' (as defined by the party) are morally superior to democratic norms and values.

---

[2] In the analyses below, ideologies and attitudes will be identified with initial caps (e.g., Racism, and Immigration), so as to distinguish them from other (e.g., non-political, non-ideological meanings or uses, or as topics of discourse).

Interestingly, as is often the case for religious ideologies and parties of the right, such 'disobedience' is contradictory with the norms and values of authoritarianism, in which God is placed superior to human and especially political entities such as governments and parliaments and their laws.

The rest of the 'Principles' text of the Republican Party details the ideologically based attitudes, as follows (henceforth, Attitudes are headlined with italics):

Abortion/Euthanasia

(3) 'The Republican Party is born from and for people and defends their life from conception to natural death.'

As the first section of this text, this attitude is dominant, and its formulation crucial for the party. Since 'People have been created with a transcendental purpose', implying a religious purpose, their 'dignity and rights' are 'prior and superior to those of the State.' In other words, as we have seen above, a radical Catholic/Christian ideology holds that religious principles are superior to political ones, thus defining a political positioning of the party at the radical right. The Republican politics about abortion in Chile should also be seen against the background of a long history of prohibition, and of a 'politics of moral sin' (Blofield, 2006).

As a brief, and in the context irrelevant, point, it is added that the party believes in 'the essential equality between men and women', a value that is further ignored in the text, which also characterizes the party as a conservative party. The attitude is now explicitly formulated as follows:

(4)   And as a direct consequence of the transcendent and dignified nature of all people, is that we defend their life from conception to natural death, without exceptions, being absolutely opposed to abortion in all its forms, euthanasia, or any action that directly seeks the artificial interruption of human life.

The detailed discourse structure of this sentence not only is in the form of an argumentation and its premise ('the transcendent and dignified nature of all people'), but also in a hyperbolic rhetorical structure ('without exceptions', 'absolutely', 'all its forms') that defines the attitude as the *radical* position of the Republican Party. The formal style of this example matches the formality of the topic and the argumentation characteristic of this election programme – in everyday speeches and parliamentary debates, politicians of RR parties would no doubt use a more 'popular' style, often associated with RR-populism.

Strangely, the fragment on the topic of abortion and euthanasia also features principles that seem to counterbalance the undemocratic position on these topics, with a general claim to democracy and human rights, a very typical ambiguity observed in many studies of RR-discourse (see, e.g., Bull & Simon-Vandenbergen, 2014; Wodak, 2021).

(5)   In this regard, the Republican Party of Chile maintains its commitment to strengthening democracy and respecting, guaranteeing and promoting the human rights guaranteed in the Constitution.

However, after this obvious disclaimer follows the following aspect of the attitude on such topics as abortion and euthanasia:

(6)   (...) in international treaties ratified and in force in Chile, and in laws. We also maintain that any foreign intervention by bodies to which Chile has not ceded, in a sovereign manner, any competence to pronounce on these matters, lacks an opinion and decision binding on our country, and therefore such opinions or decisions cannot, therefore, overlap with the rights guaranteed by our legal system.

This is a classical definition of the attitude of National Autonomy as a main application of a main value (sovereignty) of the ideology of Nationalism, in this case specifically as an argument of national views on abortion, superior to internationally shared ideologies and attitudes. This formulation also expresses the polarizing Us vs. Them structure of the ideology of Nationalism, again with an argumentative structure ('. . . and therefore . . . '). The same section argues in general in terms of the values of 'equality and dignity' but does not explain how these are relevant for the prohibition of abortion and euthanasia.

Religion

The next section is headed: 'In the Republican Party we believe in God.', but this headline seems to be contradicted by the statement that the party is non-confessional, and that any person can join. Such a discursive strategy is interesting for ideological analysis, because fundamental party texts on the one hand profess their ideology (in this case Catholicism), as already implicit in the main topic of abortion, and on the other hand don't want to exclude possible members or voters. Of course, it is added that such persons should not act 'against the dignity and transcendent purpose of persons' (e.g., read: abortion) and respect the religious discourse of the party, formulated most explicitly as follows:

(7)   Any intolerance, persecution or violence against faith in God and its expressions constitutes an act against the rights of individuals, an attack on democratic society and seriously contravenes our Western Christian tradition.

In other words, criticizing religion and its practices does not seem to be a form of the democratic value of the freedom of expression, but on the contrary an attack on democracy, on the one hand, and 'Western Christian tradition' on the other hand. For ideological analysis it is interesting and relevant to observe that the ideological norms and values of democracy may be converted into those of a religious regime or culture (for details, see also Lamour, 2022).

Family

After a discussion of the main attitude of Abortion/Euthanasia, the overall Catholic/Christian ideology at the basis of the text also pays attention to the well-known Catholic attitude of the Family, and implicitly against egalitarian matrimony:

(8) Every person is born in a social context, of human relationships, which manifests itself in the basic cell of society: the family founded on marriage between a man and a woman.

As is the case for the text and the structure of the attitude, also this belief is defended in terms of a (non-religious) argument about rights:

(9) For this reason, we believe that, based on this family ideal, children have the right to have a father and a mother, so society must make every effort to create the conditions for the exercise of this right. It is precisely in society and its interaction with others that the human person reaches his maximum possible material and spiritual development.

At the same time, there is a normative element in this attitude and its formulation in the text: 'The State must (...) protect and promote the family, the fundamental nucleus of society.'

Gender

Above, we already commented on the next main topic, namely the mysteriously vague formulation on 'objective realities', 'moral virtues', 'common sense' and the 'natural order of things', implying the Catholic view on 'gender ideologies', also against political decision-making and scientific (and medical) evidence. Such an attitude is further sustained by a historical argument, but without showing how it applies to the debate on gender:

(10) The Republican Party maintains that neither truth nor good can be defined by circumstantial majorities, because in that case we would be talking about essentially transitory, relative and changing concepts, a criterion used by those who founded the regimes that executed the greatest crimes that humanity has experienced in modern times. Our political action is aimed at speaking with truth and common sense, as well as in defense and promotion of the objective good, although this means us, on several occasions, going against the current and being unpopular communicationally. Each affiliate assumes the commitment to

speak the truth and in defense of this objective good, without complexes and without concessions.

This example defines the ideological and political position of the Republican Party: a combination of vague general values (*truth*, *good*, etc.), common sense, vague references to political opposition (circumstantial majorities), delegitimation of opponents by association (*regimes that executed the greatest crimes of humanity*), and ignoring democratic principles and the consensus (*being unpopular*), implicitly revindicating eternal (religious) truth against worldly notions (*essentially transitory, relative and changing concepts*). The text here reminds of the sermon of a (very conservative) priest.

The Fatherland

Whereas most attitudes discussed or implied by the 'Principles' text depend on the religious ideology of Catholicism, another characteristic ideology of the radical right is Nationalism (and Patriarchy), typically specified by attitudes about the Fatherland (Patria) defined as a 'community' and its history of founders, its values and traditions.

Not a single word on the multi-ethnic nature of the Chilean Nation, such as the presence of the Mapuche people and other ethnic minorities. In other words, the ideology of foundational texts not only is defined by its explicit or implied ideology and attitudes, but also by their absence, e.g., as a definition of Chile as a multinational or multiethnic state – a definition that was at stake during the debate on the referendum on a new Chilean constitution in 2022.

Social Justice

It is within this religiously defined state and its families that the text also formulates a more social attitude about 'Social Justice' for those who have been marginalized and excluded, and in which all people contribute according to their possibilities. However, to make sure this may sound as a progressive, and even a socialist attitude, there is an obvious neoliberal condition on welfare:

(11)   One of our main commitments is to make Chile a country free of all poverty, and the evils associated with it, but always with a view to each person being able to develop autonomously and that all Chileans can obtain their maximum possible material and spiritual development, on equal terms, without falling into state assistance.

Social Market Economy

Not surprisingly, this brief afterthought on welfare is followed by the topic/attitude on the Social Market Economy, the major attitude of Neoliberalist ideology:

(12) Republicans believe in a Social Market Economy.
      From the foregoing follows our resolute and fierce defense of free private
   initiative in economic matters, our defense of constitutional guarantees in order
   to prevent the State from invading the field of economic and social activity
   proper to individuals, and our defense and promotion of the right to property for
   all, because we are convinced that private property. As a result of the exercise of
   human freedom, it constitutes one of the pillars of a genuinely free and
   responsible society.

Few of the RR-parties are as explicit and detailed on the main thesis and central
value (*freedom*) of Neoliberalism, formulated also in rhetorically strong terms
of their ideological struggle (*resolute and fierce defense*) and metaphors
(*pillars*).

Democracy

One might assume that the democratic nature of the State should be the first and
main point of a fundamental text, but here appears only as 10th topic. It is defended
as the best system for the participation of its citizens and organizations, but of
course 'also preventing the promotion of social antagonisms or class struggle.'.
Without detailing the criteria of democracy, rather, the text continues with one of
the prominent topoi of populist discourse: the possible corruption at the Top:

(13) A public administration conceived as electoral booty, as an ideological trench or as
   a payer of political services, which accumulates officials and gigantic expenses,
   without an objective system of measuring the productivity of its work or functions,
   is undoubtedly a source of abuse, corruption and waste of public resources, which
   is ethically unacceptable and contrary to democracy.

Violence

The radical right is specifically interested in dealing with violence, though
limited to delinquency, terrorism, and drug trafficking as a menace for democracy. Obviously, violence by the State and its organs, such as military and police
are not even mentioned, despite the recent history of dictatorship. Rather, the
text formulates the 'ideological violence' of movements and 'social agitation'
to obtain power. It thus implicitly refers to the protest movements of students in
2019 that had given rise to major political events including elections, attempts
to change the constitution of the Pinochet era, and the election of a leftist
president Gabriel Boric on 11 March 2022 (see, e.g., Palacios-Valladares,
2020; see also the discourse analytical studies of this student movement, e.g.,
Cárdenas-Neira & Pérez-Arredondo, 2021). The metaphorical evaluation of the
student protest hardly leaves any doubt:

(14) A national agreement is needed to combat these scourges with full force and to anticipate the continued spread of these evils throughout the country.

Again, missing at this point is the well-known violence of the State in the form of the excessive force of the national police, the Caribineros, resulting in 34 deaths and 500 wounded protesters in 2020 (according to a Senate committee). Indeed, the Law and Order attitude of the radical right never applies to the State and its agencies, especially as governed by the right.

A Minimal State

At the end of the Principles text, we finally find the attitude on Decentralization, a prominent political value, in general inconsistent with the centralized tendencies of nationalism, as is the case in Spain (see further). At the same time, as a prominent attitude of a Neoliberal ideology, the text advocates a Minimal State.

Such an attitude connects well with the last Attitude of the 'Principles' text, in which the populist topos of corruption and the 'cast of privileged' and the 'powerful who live of the bureaucracy' are mentioned, that is, those who do not work for the value of the 'common good' repeatedly formulated in the text. This attitude on the State is interesting because of its populist (*caste*) implications:

(15) Linked to the above, is that we do not accept that politicians and public employees become a caste of privileged, and we rebel against the abuses of those powerful who live from bureaucracy, because we expect from the State and public services, honesty, a job well done, social responsibility, spirit of service, respect for the fundamental rights of its citizens, and an effective commitment to the common good.

But apparently such an attitude is not understood as 'populist':

(16) The Republican Party rejects populism and we promote honesty as a platform for political action.

It is thus how the programme of the Republican Party is wrapped up in a series of universal values: honesty, responsibility, efficiency, commitment and honesty.

3.1.2 Partido Republicano: Conclusions

Summarizing the ideological analysis of the Chilean radical right Republican Party, we have found the main ideology of conservative Catholicism and its attitudes about Abortion, Euthanasia, Gay Marriage, and Family Values, and some Nationalist and Neoliberal attitudes about Freedom of Enterprise and a Small State. The attitude about violence is limited to foreign and anti-state violence, such as terrorism, drug trafficking and protest movements, within authoritarian values. Racism is not explicit as an ideology (for instance through anti-immigration Attitudes), but implicit by the absence of the very mention of the Mapuche people, the multi-ethnic nation and multiculturalism. Compared with for instance the electoral programme in the Netherlands, the style of the text – lexical items, sentence structure – is rather formal.

3.2 Spain: Vox

Vox was founded in 2013 as a radical separation from the conservative Popular Party (PP) and led by Santiago Abascal. In the general elections of 2018, it obtained 15.09 per cent of the votes, but in the elections of 2023 it dropped to 12.39 per cent of the vote. In this study I focus only on the ideologies as formulated in the Electoral Programme 2023 (see especially also Ferreira, 2019).

The analysis does not detail the electoral history, the political activities, or the historical background of the party and many of the current political events in which Vox is involved. These have been discussed in a large number of newspaper articles, books and academic and journalistic articles in Spanish and some in English (see, e.g., Barrio, De Oger & Field, 2021; Fernández Sánchez, 2019; Ferreira, 2019; Garrido Rubia & Mora, 2020; Olmeda Gómez, 2020; Rama et al., 2020). Also because of many more scholarly studies, the analysis of their programme will be more detailed than that of the other radical right parties analysed in the study.

3.2.1 The Electoral Programme of Vox

The electoral programme of Vox was published on the website of Vox in voxespana.es as preparation for the national elections of July 28, 2023, unexpectedly planned by Prime Minister Pedro Sánchez, after significant losses of his socialist party (PSOE) in the local elections of May 2023. In the national elections the Right (PP and Vox) only obtained 171 seats in parliament, 5 too little to be able to govern with a majority of 176 seats in parliament of 350 seats. In these elections Vox lost 18 of its 56 seats.

An electoral programme is a foundational discourse genre, as is also the case for manifestos (Budge, 2015; Van Dijk, 2023b, 2023c). Its structures and strategies express the ideologies, planned policies, and bills of the party, which depend also on the current social political situation.

As is the case for the study of the RR-party in Chile, the analysis will be an *ideological analysis*, not a detailed discourse analysis, which would examine the vast complexity of grammatical, semantic, pragmatic, rhetorical, argumentative, narrative, and ideological structures. Only those (mostly semantic) structures will be studied that are manifestations of underlying ideologies and attitudes and their categories, and some structures that directly index underlying ideologies and attitudes.

The programme consists of 20 chapters, 175 pages, and 28,187 words. Its title is *Un Programa Para Lo Que Importa* (A program for What Matters), with the subtitle *Programa Electoral para las Elecciones Generales 23 de julio de 2023* (Electoral Program for the General Elections July 23, 2023). The cover features a page-length picture of party leader Santiago Abascal.

The twenty chapters are variously entitled in terms of the major attitudes/ issues or values of the ideologies of Vox, such as Equality among Spaniards, the Unity of Spain, the 'depolitization' of Justice, and the usual social domains of politics and society: Education, Employment and Salaries, Housing, Health, Security and Defence, European Union, the Environment ('Green Spain') and Family issues. Each of these 'chapters' consists of a political introduction, followed by 'Medidas' (Measures, Policies) and Actions (proposals of Bills).

The style and rhetoric of the programme is characteristic of an electoral programme. This means that it is more formal than parliamentary debates and much less rhetorical than posts on social media or public speeches of Vox politicians. On the other hand, an electoral programme, is part of a political debate, e.g., between the conservative and radical right opposition against the leftist government of socialist PSOE and radical left Podemos. Different from the other RR-discourses analysed in this study, this means that each chapter is prefaced with an explicit attack against socialist Prime Minister Pedro Sánchez, before formulating the summary of a major topic or domain and details of the policies and bills of Vox. This discourse structure is characteristic of Vox's political style, which is explicitly antagonistic against the (leftist) government, in particular, and against liberal ideas and policies, in general, defining Vox especially as a Reactionary party, as defined above. I distinguish between general ideologies and more specific attitudes by printing ideologies in **bold italics** and attitudes in *italics*.

Nationalism

No doubt Nationalism is the main ideology of the ideological cluster of Vox. It is expressed in nearly all topics of the twenty chapters, and most explicitly formulated in the first two chapters on Spanish people and Spain as a country and combined with other ideologies in the discussion of attitudes about major issues. This means that many attitudes expressed in the programme appear as specifications of several ideologies below. For instance, the attitude on immigration will appear as an attitude of both Nationalism and Racism as founding ideologies of Vox.

Nationalism as an ideology has been studied in a vast number of studies, also within discourse studies (see, e.g., Wodak, 2009), not to be reviewed here. Nationalism in Spain is an ideology broadly shared, especially at the right. It features various beliefs defining the respective categories of the Nationalist ideology: about (i) 'our' country, state, people, history, and relations with other nations/countries, collectively defining our Identity; (ii) what WE do or should do; (iii) with what Goals; with (iv) what Norms and Values, and with our Allies and against Our Enemies. Though very general, Nationalism as an ideology may take various forms in different social, political, and historical contexts. In contemporary Spain, it is influenced by the earlier dictatorship of Franco (and resistance against it), colonial history, dominant Catholic religion, the organization of autonomous regions, the relationship with the European Union, and the socio-economic aspects of the country, and especially its relative poverty. These variable aspects of Spanish nationalism also are defined by other ideologies and attitudes.

Anti-Separatism, Anti-Regionalism

Within the nationalist ideology of Vox, the main ideological attitude may best be called Anti-Separatism or more generally Anti-Regionalism, an attitude that actually motivated the very foundation of the party by those politicians of the conservative PP who are most radically opposed against separate autonomous regions. This applies especially in Catalonia and Basque country, with their own language, parliament, police, and regional organizations of education and health services.

This radical ideological and political opposition against the autonomous regions was especially exacerbated by the (illegal) independence declaration by independence parties in Catalonia in 2017. Large parts of the discourse and the policies of the radical right use this event as proof of the necessity of radical forms of anti-separatism. Such positioning was electorally relevant because within Catalonia itself and more generally throughout Spain there was widespread opposition against Catalan independence (Arroyo Menéndez, 2020).

The general attitude of Anti-Separatism is specified by a large number of partial attitudes in many social and political domains, such as education, health, and security, and in general the regional administration. Throughout the electoral programme, detailed policies and bills are the expression of these nationalist attitudes against separatism and more generally against the very power of the autonomous regions.

Within this general framework, the first chapter of the programme begins as follows:

(17)   Pedro Sánchez will be remembered as the president who was hard and implacable with honest Spaniards and soft on criminals, enemies of Spain and foreign elites. His concessions to separatism and his commitment to a multilevel Spain has only benefited the regional elites and has allowed the consolidation of an unjust model that hampers the prosperity and welfare of the Spanish people.

This example shows that the formulation of an electoral programme not only is an expression of ideologies and its attitudes, but especially also part of a political battle, featuring an attack of the opponent, consisting of serious accusations. However, besides this usual move of election discourse, the ideological point of the accusation is of course its Nationalist ideology and the negative attitudes about Separatism and Internationalism, rhetorically emphasized by specific lexical items (*hard, implacable, enemies, criminals,* etc.) and polarization (*hard* vs. *soft*). Notice that the example not only expresses and reproduces nationalist attitudes but also racist ones by associating foreigners with crime and enemies, which at the same time has the authoritarian expression of being soft on crime of a Law-and-Order attitude. We see that the same example may be an expression of various ideologies and attitudes.

At the same time, this fragment features an example of the polarizing *populist discourse strategy* pitching of (honest) Spanish people on the one hand and foreign and regionalist elites, on the other hand, the discourse strategy generally considered to be defining populism (but see our critical analysis of such theories above). Vox thus strategically positions itself as the defender of 'the honest (Spanish) people' against its ideological opponents (THEM), following the usual ingroup-outgroup polarization of the ideology.

Centralism and Unification

Another attitude of Nationalism is not only an attack on separatism, independence and regionalism, but at the same time a counter-political model of centralism and unification (the title of the chapter):

(18)   Far from bringing the administrations closer to the citizens, the autonomous state has only served to impose new centralisms that seek an artificial homogenisation and that threaten the rich diversity of Spain and its provincial plurality, erecting artificial barriers between Spaniards and imposing an administrative chaos contrary to solidarity between people and territories.

Again, the discourse strategy is a populist move pitching (Spanish) citizens against the autonomous state, but also formulating the (positive) values of the alternative (a unified Spain): diversity, plurality and solidarity, typical positive, liberal values. That the proposed alternative (unification and centralism) is precisely a contradiction of such values remains of course implicit in such discourse. Though not the topic of this study, notice also the formal style, the long sentence and lexical choice (e.g., *homogenisation*) of the programme, on the one hand, with much less formal expressions of a political attack (*chaos*).

Example (18) is a discursive expression of an underlying Attitude that also might provide ideas about the cognitive organization of attitudes: on the one hand the usual polarization between Us and Them, and on the other hand an *argumentative structure* why autonomous regions are bad – and against the people. The example is followed by a long list of policies and ideas for bills aiming to diminish or even delete many forms of autonomous structures, even those described in the constitution. Many of the following chapters, e.g., on education and health further specify this form of unification and centralization. That these are not just ideas or policies, but actual forms of government was shown after the 2023 election in those provinces where Vox governed with the PP.

Spain as Nation and Homeland

Although the first concern of Vox is the opposition against separatism, independence, and regionalism, its ideas on unification and centralization presuppose an attitude about Spain as a Nation, the kernel of Nationalism, the Homeland (Patria):

(19) Spain is a reality that transcends the Spaniards of a certain time and place; It is an inheritance received from our ancestors that we must take care of and improve to bequeath it to the next generations. Our homeland is the guarantee of rights and equality, especially of the most vulnerable.

We see that the metaphysical idea of the Nation is metaphorically defined as an inheritance, indeed a 'patrimony' that can be bequeathed by 'our' ancestors. Notice that such a formulation (*our ancestors, next generations*) implies that the Nation cannot be bequeathed to immigrants, an implication of the Racist ideology combined with nationalism in the Nativist ideological cluster. The historical nature of the Fatherland is a well-known topos of RR discourse (Wodak, 2009, 2021).

Interestingly, here and elsewhere in the text, Vox only uses the masculine grammatical form *los españoles*, and not, as other parties today do, both the masculine and the feminine form *los españoles y las españolas*, a form of inclusion no doubt associated with a progressive, feminist ideologies, but now adopted more generally in political and other public discourse in Spain. In other words, the discursive manifestation of ideology is also marked in the grammar, in this case combining Nationalism with Sexism/Patriarchy/Antifeminism. The feminine form is only used as adjective to mention Spanish families, enterprises, and cities. Next we examine in more detail the discursive expression of the machismo-patriarchy ideology of Vox.

We now have all ingredients of the Nationalist configuration of the Unity of Spain in terms of concepts of 'enemies', 'traitors', 'alien', 'foreign' as opposed to the 'needs' of the Spaniards. The text thus construes a clear ideological polarization between Us, the Spaniards (and the National Interest) vs. Them, the Autonomous Regions as aliens, whose citizens by implication are not categorized as Spaniards, and their needs as irrelevant. That the organization of the State in autonomous regions is defined in the Constitution is obviously not mentioned. As we have seen above, the discursive expression of ideologies is also characterized by what is explicitly left out or silenced. With this definition of the Nation, the goal of this nationalist Attitude is obvious:

(20)   It is urgent to recover for the common project of Spain those thousands of compatriots who have sentimentally disassociated themselves from the Nation, spurred on by the ideological indoctrination of separatism and globalism.

Notice that at the abstract level of a formal election programme, the debate is not just in terms of specific attitudes, but even more abstractly at the level of an ideological struggle, in this case between Nationalism and what are called the ideologies of separatism and globalism. More generally, opponent attitudes or ideologies are routinely associated in the text with indoctrination, a standard (negative) attitude dominated by many ideologies (those of Religion, Nationalism, (Anti)Racism, etc.). Relevant in example (20) is also the denomination of the people of the autonomous regions in terms of the positive (ingroup) term 'compatriots', implying that the indoctrination is done by the regional elites – as is also obvious in the rest of the Program.

Anti-Globalism

Example (20) also introduces another characteristic attitude of nationalist ideologies: Anti-globalism, a widely shared attitude of the radical right in many countries (Sanahuja Perales & López Burian, 2022; Steger, 2019). Throughout the programme any aspects of society that can be associated with globalism are violently attacked, and of course associated with the left and rejected as indoctrination, implying that it must be ubiquitous in much public discourse. Indeed, if Nationalism and its attitudes define Vox, globalism is the ideology attributed to its political and ideological opponents.

The Symbols of the Nation

Nationalists pay special attention to the characteristics of the symbols of the Nation, such as the Flag, the national Anthem, and in Spain, of course, also The Crown. Such symbols must be respected, revered, and protected. Within the authoritarian system of Law and Order, this must also mean that attacks against such symbols must be severely punished:

(21) We will provide maximum legal protection to the symbols of the nation, especially the Flag, the Anthem and the Crown. The penalties for offenses and outrages against Spain and its symbols or emblems must be aggravated so that no affront to them goes unpunished.

Spanish Civilization and Colonialism

Of the many aspects of the Spanish Nation are also its language and other cultural aspects. Such is not just relevant today, but also for the past. This means that against contemporary liberal moves of de-colonization (as in some official declarations in Western Europe; see, also Kumarasingham, 2020), the radical right also celebrates its colonization as a form of bringing 'civilization' to the Americas, an attitude that specifically embodies the value of nationalist Pride. Also on this issue, the programme hardly minces words in the formulation of this reactionary attitude:

(22) We will disseminate and protect the national identity and the contribution of Spain to civilization and universal history, with special attention to the deeds and exploits of our national heroes inside and outside our borders.

      We will promote the Spanish language abroad through the Cervantes Institute, defense of the character, culture and Spanish symbols around the world; especially in Latin America.

This attitude is also typical of the radical right's cultural war as a backlash against liberal forms of national self-criticism about the crimes of the past. Heroes of the past are celebrated in radical right discourse (Kelsey, 2016). Topoi such as the glorious past and its heroes are also aspects of the nostalgia of RR discourse (for nostalgia of Vox, see Fernández Riquelme, 2020; for the role of history for Vox, see Ballester Rodríguez, 2021, 2023).

Revisionism

The celebration of colonialism is obviously also a denial of the many crimes of the past, such as racism and colonial exploitation, a form of revisionism that is a very frequent attitude of nationalisms in several European countries (Valencia-García, 2020).

Such revisionism not only applies to the colonial past, but also to the political present: the attitudes about the recent Franco dictatorship. Vox's political heritage is closely associated with its ideologies and parties (e.g., the *falange*). Hence, any political initiative to investigate the crimes of the dictatorship, as is the case in the law of Democratic Memory, is violently opposed, and threatened with abolition as soon as Vox will be in power:

(23)   We will repeal all laws that the Sánchez government has passed or maintained and encourage confrontation and division among Spaniards, such as the Democratic Memory Law or the LGTBI Law.

Instead, Vox will promote a special Law for the victims of the terrorism of the Basque ETA:

(24)   We will promote the approval of a Law of Memory, Dignity and Justice for the Victims of Terrorism. This rule will effectively prevent the glorification of terrorism, tributes to terrorists, acts of humiliation of the victims or attacks on the institutions and symbols of Spain.

Despite strengthening of all organizations of Law and Order (see further), nationalist ideologies hardly celebrate policies that call national and international attention to the history of the national crimes of the dictatorship. So, the Law of 'Democratic Memory', organizing increased knowledge of the dictatorship, is too close for comfort for a party whose historical and political roots, ideologies and policies remind those of the Franco regime. Different from what happened in other countries, such as Truth Committees in Germany, South Africa, Chile, or Argentina, Vox does not want to focus on that truth. Aligned with its general attack on all forms of terrorism, it rather focuses on the (past) terrorism of ETA, and the coalition of the socialist governments with Basque political parties.

Racism

Closely related to nationalism is the ideology of Racism, including Xenophobia, Islamophobia and Antisemitism (among many studies, see Van Dijk, 1993). We have seen that the Nation is defined for Spanish people, and hence excludes immigrants and minorities. Together with Nationalism, Racism is the most widespread ideology in Europe and all Europeanized countries (Australia, New Zealand, the United States, and large parts of Latin America), and shared by nearly all their parties and organizations of the radical right.

Of course, with the growth of antiracism and its discourses (Van Dijk, 2021a), explicit Racism is often no longer 'politically correct', even on the Right, but its many contemporary forms, e.g., of cultural racism, and especially as presupposed by anti-immigrant policies, is widely shared by radical and extremist right parties and organizations. As has often been observed in other studies, the ideologies of Racism and Nationalism define a cluster often called Nativism (but recall that this ideology cluster is not itself an ideology). Without entering in the vast field of theories of racism and racist discourse (see Solomos, 2020), we focus here only on the ideological attitudes specifically formulated in the Electoral Programme of Vox, attitudes that are widely shared in other countries.

Compared to other countries, Spain for many years seemed like an exception on the role of radical right parties in general, and on Racism in particular, even on the Right. However, together with the topic of Catalan independence, Vox soon understood that is a topic with which to get a substantial popular vote.

Immigration

The main Attitude based on a racist ideology, also in Spain, is about the ubiquitous and most controversial issue of immigration (see, e.g., Castro Martínez & Mo Groba, 2020; Suárez, 2021). As in other countries, the populist strategy of Vox is to blame the current government, especially on the left, to 'let in' thousands of migrants and refugees. Also in Spain, that populist strategy is to portray poor workers and families as the victims of immigration and the 'privileged elites'. This is how the chapter on immigration is opened, with the usual populist strategy to polarize the (leftist) government with ordinary people:

(25) Pedro Sánchez and his government have been allies and promoters of all globalist policies and multiculturalism that bet on the disorderly arrival of millions of illegal immigrants. The consequences have not been suffered by those who have imposed these policies from their offices and mansions with private security, but by Spanish families who suffer insecurity and degradation in their neighbourhoods.

We see in this first statement on immigration how the topic is associated with the nationalist attitude on Globalism, the authoritarian attitude of Law and Order, and negative topics of illegality, disorder, insecurity and degradation – and hence not with the multiple cultural and economic contributions of immigrants. This form of discursive racism has been observed in a very large number of books and articles, especially since the 1980s (Van Dijk, 1993).

In an official programme of 2023, Vox can hardly blame and attack all immigrants (indeed thousands may have Spanish nationality and might vote), so the preferred ones are those who have or search for a job and adapt themselves to Spanish culture.

Instead of detailed analysis of the relevant fragments of the electoral pro-gramme, it suffices to list Vox's specific attitudes and policies within its nationalist-racist ideology cluster, attitudes that each would deserve an article or a whole book:

- As is often the case in the programme, a national referendum on immigration is proposed.
- Foreign youth must be repatriated with their parent to their country of origin.
- Illegal immigrants cannot be inscribed in the municipal register.
- Multiculturalism ('failed in North Europa') is anathema.
- Illegal and criminal immigrants should be expelled.
- Assistance to illegal immigrant should not be financed.
- Punishment of 'illegal immigration mafias' should be strengthened.
- Policies that attract immigrants should be stopped.
- Culturally closer immigrants from Latin America should be preferred.
- A Naval blockade should be established against boats of illegal immigrants.
- With Europe regions outside of Europe should house refugees.

Integration

Whereas much of the racist discourse of the radical right focuses on immigration and how such immigration, especially of 'illegal' immigrants, should be blocked, once they have arrived in Spain, don't go back, and cannot be sent back, a major attitude is Integration, especially in other countries in Europe with much earlier migration. Where immigration itself is associated with Law-and-Order topics such as 'illegal' immigrants, Integration is primarily a cultural attitude, of course presupposing that by definition immigrants have an alien culture. It also presupposes that all people in Spain have the same culture, and it implies that integration is the task of the immigrants, not of the autochthonous population:

(26) Those immigrants who have arrived legally in Spain with the intention of working, integrating and contributing to the development of the nation that welcomes them are also victims of those politicians, associations and international organizations that are actively collaborating with the mafias of human trafficking, and who profit thanks to the devastating goodwill of the elites.

(27) Anyone who wants to come and stay in Spain in search of opportunities must comply with the law and have a clear will to integrate and adapt.

Islam

As is the case in other European countries, such as France, Germany, the UK, the Netherlands, and the Scandinavian countries, immigration is often associated with Islam and Muslims. That issue not only is related to topics such as cultural adaptation (such as not wearing a hijab, or topics related to mosques), but also with more negative Islamophobia, such as associating Muslim immigrants with the oft repeated Law-and-Order topic of terrorism:

(28) Relentless fight against terrorism. Those responsible for the Islamic religion in Spain will be required to collaborate in the arrest of radicals. Spain will participate in international security missions and the fight against jihadism according to our interests and capabilities.

Whether or not as terrorist 'jihadism', and always related to issues of integration, the Islamophobic variant of Racism will focus on 'Islamic Fundamentalism', whether or not such radicalism is widespread in the Islamic community.:

(29) Zero tolerance for all forms of Islamic fundamentalism. We will close mosques or places of worship that propagate ideas that are contrary to our culture and identity such as Islamic radicalism, jihad or contempt for women and our customs.

As may be expected, the racist opposition of the radical right against Islamist radicalism is itself radical (*zero tolerance, close mosques,* etc.), also in the nationalist defence of 'our culture and identity', of course assumed to be superior. Remarkable in example (29) is the surprising occurrence of 'women', a word and notion nearly absent in the programme and hence as marginalized by Vox as much as assumed to be in Islam.

Neoliberalism

Political parties on the Right, and hence also a radical right party such as Vox, usually are in favour of attitudes based on Neoliberalism, and hence as opposed to typical Socialist attitudes. As is the case for many of the inconsistencies between ideologies or attitudes, such is also the case for the well-known populist claim that the radical right is the champion of the People. If such were right, it would be closer to the radical left (such as that of Podemos), and its ideological (and not just discursive) opposition against the economic elites, such as banks. So, let's see how Vox manages the topic of work and related social-economic issues.

Jobs

As may be expected, the electoral programme of Vox features the usual attitudes of a neoliberal ideology – and policies. As is often the case, also these attitudes are controlled by several underlying ideologies. For instance, the topic of jobs is controlled by Nationalism, Racism, and Neoliberalism: Here is the way the programme starts its ideas on work in Spain:

(30)   The employment of Spaniards is the basis of their well-being and freedom. The families of workers and self-employed have been suffering for years from the policies of fiscal suffocation, the relocation of companies and the general drop in wages.

Such a formulation may be, and has been, used by any party, on the left and the right, and the ideological problem then is how Vox as a party of the radical right positions itself against a leftist government and its laws and policies. One element in this formulation that gives a hint is that of 'fiscal suffocation', a vague formal term used to describe high(er) taxes, which in this case implicates a classical neoliberal policy to lower taxes. The way to attack leftist policies obviously is not to mention its policies in favour of poor people, but to continue the nationalist topic, in this case against the forms of 'internationalism' or 'globalism', e.g., as follows:

(31)   (. . .) socialist and globalist policies the access and quality of jobs in Spain: destruction of our industry (. . .) unfair foreign competition, uncontrolled immigration, gender quotas and an ultimatum between a decent salary or being able to dedicate time to a family. Faced with this, the ultra-subsidized unions, instead of defending the workers, have betrayed them to preserve their privileges, becoming lackeys of the government and whitewashing the precariousness that Spaniards suffer today.

We see how at the radical right the precariousness of labour is redefined is terms of the following ideologies and attitudes: Nationalism (foreign competition), Racism (uncontrolled immigration), Patriarchy (gender quotas), and Family values. Neoliberalism itself is formulated in terms of the classical Anti-Union Attitude, negatively presented as 'lackeys' and as the enemy of the workers and the Spanish people within the usual populist polarization between the (socialist, union, etc.) elites and the (hardworking) people. But in the Nativist ideology cluster of Nationalism and Racism combined with Neoliberalism, 'foreign' workers are not included: 'Behind every worker there is a Spaniard (. . .) We will protect Spanish workers.'

Obviously, in a text about and addressed to the workers, this neoliberal introduction only can plan to lower taxes and raise wages. However, since this may destroy labour, the businesses need to pay less taxes, consistent with neoliberalist attitudes. How in such a situation the (social) policies of the State are financed, Vox has recourse to the usual populist topos of the corrupt elites, this time at the left ('activists'):

(32)   In Spain there are poverty wages and unacceptable unemployment because everyone's work sustains the welfare state of politicians and their paid activists.

Besides the unexplained existence of 'paid activists', another crucial issue is the negatively presented 'welfare state', a typical social-democratic invention incompatible with the neoliberal radical right, in this case associated not with those for whom it serves but with the politicians whose propose its policies. Again, what is not said here is perhaps most relevant, namely that most politicians associated with corruption, as shown in many processes, were those of the conservative right of the Partido Popular, and not the Left.

Within the same Neoliberal ideology, we may of course expect not only an attack of the Unions, but also of strikes, a classical neoliberal attitude:

(33)   We will effectively guarantee the right to work by prohibiting coercive actions in political strikes.

The way this is formulated is an interesting discursive and ideological trick, viz. by defining the right to work to be incompatible with the right to strike, and to delegitimate strikes in terms of 'coercive actions' and 'political'. No doubt many of the 'workers' the populist text claims to protect might wonder whether the policies of Vox are in their favour or in favour of their bosses.

We have found above that some topics of the electoral programme of Vox casually introduce topics and attitudes that are at best locally incoherent, if not inconsistent. Thus, neoliberal principles and policies may be combined with nationalist ones in terms of criticizing 'globalist impositions,' on the one hand, and with anti-environmental attitudes, on the other hand, when such globalist ideas destroy 'Spanish industries'. Instead, Vox proposes to solve the problems of the environment with 'commonsense,' which means:

(34)   Protection of our economy, compatible with the economic development and well-being of Spaniards.

It is not surprising that the vast problem of the Climate Crisis, and the urgent policies it requires, does not seem to require detailed comments in this 195-page document, as is the case in general for RR discourse (Forchtner, 2020). As we have seen before, what the text does not say is often more relevant than what it does say, as is also the case in form of Negationism of the radical right. It is in this way the text often combines formulations of ideological clusters and their attitudes, here combining Neoliberalism, Nationalism. Racism, Patriarchy and Anti-Environmentalism.

For the same reasons of ideological compatibility, a section on labour needs to talk about foreign labour, and hence on immigration, but formulated with the following conditions that are topoi of racist ideological discourse:

(35) We will guarantee legal, orderly immigration adapted to the needs and possibilities of our labour market to ensure the employment of Spaniards and immigrants who, arriving legally, contribute their effort and respect our way of life.

The emphasis on legality politically implicates the racist policies of Vox against 'illegal' immigrants, mentioned earlier, the primacy of Spaniards, and the usual requirement to respect 'our way of life' as one of the topoi of cultural racism. In other words, any topic or issue of the text is systematically associated with racist nationalism (Nativism). Nationalist anti-regionalism may become relevant against any requirement by which people are required to learn the language of the autonomous regions. At the same time, labour policies may be associated with the authoritarian Law-and-Order measures of strict ('con dureza') punishment of those who employ illegal immigrants.

Housing

Neoliberalism is an ideology that applies to all aspects of society, also to the crucial topic of housing. This is a major issue in Spain, where rents are vastly higher than the average salary and controlled by the economic freedom of owners. As a party of the radical right, how does Vox manage its natural allegiance to private property and the major concerns of the people who can't pay the rent? So, who are the major threat to homeowners in Spain? Its first 'measure' gives the answer:

(36) Zero tolerance for illegal occupation. We will reform both the Criminal Code and the Criminal and Civil Procedure Laws to really and effectively protect owners who suffer the action of occupation mafias or the illegal entry of a squatter into their home. Every Spaniard must have the ability to defend himself and his loved ones against aggression in his own home.

Hence, not a protection of tenants against homeowners, but of homeowners against the notorious 'okupas', squatters, of course in a way most familiar with the radical right: by Law and Order. 'To defend himself' seems like a reasonable solution, but implies one aspect of Law and Order in Spain not spelled out in this programme: the use of violent 'anti-okupas' who are the real mafias of the housing market.

The interest of homeowners is just one aspect of neoliberal ideology. The same applies to owners and their protection against the city councils:

(37) (. . .) the release of land seized by municipalities and autonomous communities for the benefit of corrupt parties and politicians, and to ensure a correct, agile and harmonious urban development throughout Spain.

The programme often claims that policies of Vox protect the 'Common Good', but of course, such protagonism has its limits. Within another major topic of the programme, neoliberal ideology also combines with the ideology of anti-environmentalism and anti-European nationalism (Rooduijn & Van Kessel, 2019).

(38) We therefore reject globalist projects such as the so-called European New Bauhaus promoted by Brussels bureaucrats, which, with the alibi of climate fanaticism and the energy efficiency of buildings, aims to standardize the reality of our cities.

Spanish Products

Neoliberalism and Nationalism combine in the attitude about Spanish products, a major topic of the programme. Any party might claim to protect national products and services against international ones, so this should not just be a policy at the radical right. Hence, the way such a policy of preference is formulated provides insight into its ideological foundation. Nationalism in this case takes the form of typical radical right anti-globalism and combines with anti-environmentalism and anti-European populism:

(39) The globalist elites are promoting both in Brussels and in Spain and its regions ruthless environmental rules and bureaucracy that suffocate our farmers, ranchers, fishermen and industries. The consequence is the disappearance of certain productive sectors that had been supporting thousands of Spanish families for centuries, even in sectors in which Spain stood out internationally.

Such fragments not only bear witness of the underlying ideological cluster, but also highlight the obvious addressees and interests of such policies: Spanish farmers are the targeted voters of the party. As is also the case for Sweden Democrats, Vox more generally focuses on various 'rural' topics, such as the promotion of rural tourism and the conservation of 'our natural patrimony'. But self-serving nationalism is always combined with anti-globalist attitudes, even when this means rejecting international laws and regulations on nutrition (such as international labelling) and the environment:

(40) We will not allow interference from foreign countries and green lobbies that attack the Spanish product and the Spaniards who work hard to achieve it.

Lowering Taxes

The main policy of neoliberal parties, also to get part of the popular vote, especially of the middle and upper class, is of course lowering taxes. In the continuous economic crisis in Spain since 2008, such policies are easy to sell, e.g., as follows:

(41) (...) Spaniards break records in misery. Never before has the gulf between the welfare state of the elites and the harsh reality of Spaniards been greater. It is indecent that the privileges of the usual are sustained at the expense of the effort of the middle and working classes.

Such a concern for the working class, however, is short-lived. Directly following this passage, there is a concern for the companies that suffer from autonomous regions. And hence also their taxes should be lowered, as in the following metaphorically (*hell*) and hyperbolically (*radically, drastically*) enhanced excerpt:

(42) At VOX we will put an end to the fiscal and bureaucratic hell suffered by Spaniards by radically lowering all taxes and drastically cutting unnecessary political spending to boost our competitiveness and strengthen our infrastructures and public services.

No wonder that in this chapter Vox claims to 'implement the largest and most profound tax reform in recent history'. With the vast number of other economic promises of lowering taxes and special assistance (e.g., of large families), one may wonder how a Vox government would get any income at all to pay for these promises. Consistent with such policies is also the elimination of inheritance tax, of course – thus pandering to the rich rather than to poor workers.

But there are also ideas how to save money, for instance by eliminating the ministry and local departments of equality (as they already did in the summer of 2023 as soon as they got power in some provinces), not seen as relevant for women, but as typical 'chiringuitos' (literally a beach bar, but more generally and negatively for a small outfit) of the left:

(43) We will close all ideological public 'chiringuitos' irrigated with public money such as LGBT shops, historical memory shops, radical ecologists or separatists or linked to the implementation of the 2030 Agenda and we will put an end to subsidies and aid when it comes to private entities.

Such passages show explicitly what the ideological opponents of the radical right are, and what will happen (and already happens) if Vox can govern with the Popular Party.

Catholicism

Spain is traditionally a Catholic country, and any kind of Conservatism, especially at the radical right, will naturally espouse Catholicism as a guiding ideology, if only to please and capture many votes. But there are many more or less liberal or traditional forms of Catholicism. Vox, in the tradition of nationalist Catholicism of the Franco regime, defends the more traditional perspective, associated with Opus Dei, and their retrograde ideas about families, (homo)sexuality, gender, euthanasia, and the major topic of abortion. These are internationally well-known topics, issues and attitudes, and hence need no detailed analysis beyond some typical quotes.

Abortion and Euthanasia

The topic of abortion usually is associated with that of euthanasia, with which it can be combined in the positive phrase of the 'right to life':

(44) We will approve health legislation that respects the right to life and physical and moral integrity. This will include a Palliative Care Act that ensures care for people in the critical and terminal phases of life, birth and family support laws, as well as the repeal of euthanasia and abortion laws.

The electoral problem is that, also in Spain, and also among Catholics, the rights of abortion and euthanasia are widely supported by the population. Hence, different from the explicit prohibition by the radical right Republican Party in very Catholic Chile, Vox in Spain follows a more careful policy – not explicitly prohibiting abortion or euthanasia, but to provide special care for those who need it – thus implicating that such care may consist in dissuading those who might want to commit the sin of unnaturally terminating life.

The Culture War

The main ideological reaction of the radical right are the various domains of the old topic of the Culture War(s) (see, e.g., Prothero, 2016). Education is one of these domains, also in Spain. Throughout its programme nationalist attitudes are about what people should know or how children should be educated. Textbooks are a major topic of nationalist and racist concern, as has also been shown in Florida, where Governor DeSantis prohibited textbooks on sexuality, racism of Black History.

Regional Languages

In Spain, the anti-separatist attitude against any 'autonomous' issue focuses primarily on the autonomous languages, especially Catalan and Basque, and their priority, in classrooms, textbooks and public discourse. Moreover, children should not focus on local histories, but on nationalist ones. The keyword in the chapter is *indoctrination*:

(45) the degradation that education has been suffering in Spain in recent decades due to the autonomous state, ideological indoctrination in schools and universities, and successive educational laws, which have ceased to promote excellence and quality.

Education

The nationalist opposition against the important role of the local languages is not just a question of nationalist centralism of Spanish ('national cohesion'), but the ideological reaction of the radical right against the left, also in education:

(46) We will approve a lasting National Education Law that establishes common contents and whose maxim is to make education an engine of personal development of our youth and an element of national cohesion, far from the sectarianism and radical ideological imposition that have allowed and promoted the parties of progressive consensus.

Another topic of the chapter on education is the thesis that not the schools or the teachers, but the parents should decide what children should learn:

(47) Direct attack on the constitutional freedom of parents to educate their children according to their moral convictions, to the point of openly stating that 'children do not belong to parents.'

The claimed authority of the parents not only is a question of morality, but it is also political, as is the case in the following accusation: '(..) The presence in the classroom of activists and associations that seek to ideologically indoctrinate children by going over the authority of their parents.' Vox thus styles itself as the powerful ('with extreme harshness') protector of the 'innocent',

(48) We will guarantee by law the protection of school-age minors, punishing with extreme harshness the activities of indoctrination and corruption that attempt against their innocence.

Thus, the culture war is mainly an ideological war, protecting not only children but also students against what is defined as 'political correctness':

(49) The University must be rescued from all totalitarian ideological impositions and its culture of cancellation, recovering its vocation as a space of freedom and search for truth and beauty. We will guarantee the academic freedom of teachers in the classroom against the impositions of political correctness.

Notice the ubiquitous presuppositions in such fragments about what happens in the universities. As is the case in the international debate of the radical right, Vox also must fight against the alleged 'culture of cancellation' attributed to the left. Ironically, the verbs most frequent of the election programme are the 'cancelling' acts of a vast number of laws and regulations: *derogar* (to repeal), *rechazar* (to reject).

Textbooks

The centralist-nationalist ideology against most of the properties of the autonomous regions is not just a question of language or independence 'indoctrination' but also a struggle about the contents of teaching and textbooks, which obviously will not only be about the 'regions' but about the history and symbols of 'Hispanicity':

(50) We will include in the curricula content on the history of Spain, national identity and the contribution of Spain to civilization and universal history, with special attention to the deeds and exploits of our national heroes, as well as to the symbols of the Nation, especially the Flag, the Anthem and the Crown. Knowledge of the cultural manifestations of our Nation and Hispanidad will also be promoted.

Vox thus plans a bill that will promote the teaching of the humanities, especially featuring the 'cultural tradition of Spain and the rest of the West', highlighting such conservative values as effort and discipline. Besides Nationalism and its values, such teaching will also be Catholic: the children will get the 'religious and moral formation according to the beliefs' of the parents. And yet, at the same time, such teaching should be 'ideologically neutral'.

Gender

Another major topic of the Culture Wars started by the radical right is gender (Dietze & Roth, 2020; Kottig, 2016). So, within the topic of security, the controversial law on gender violence will be repealed. The very 'ideological' notion of 'gender' should rather be abolished, because according to the scientific truth of the international radical right and a Catholic ideology, there are only men and women. Within the same framework, no special departments or commissariats are necessary for women or violence against women. These are just 'family matters'.

Since according to Catholic doctrine, there is no such thing as 'gender', but only commonsense notions such as women and men, one would expect at least a chapter on women. However, we have seen that, in Spanish, Spanish women (*españolas*) are hardly mentioned in the programme. Instead, they are grammatically part of the masculine form 'los españoles'), contrary to widespread usage in Spain.

Violence against women in Spain, where at least 50 women are assassinated each year, for Vox may not be called 'machista' or even 'gender violence', but is 'family violence', because it happens that occasionally also men are victims of such violence, and hence need protection, an argument of most pure machismo ideology (see also Vanegas, 2021; for 'manliness' at the radical right, see also Keil, 2020).

(51)   We will repeal the Comprehensive Law on Gender Violence, which enshrines criminal asymmetry and inequality between men and women and undermines the basic pillars of the rule of law.

Anti-Environmentalism and Negationism

Against the internationally growing urgency of the climate crisis and ubiquitous green policies, it is hard to defend radical right ideologies of denial (see Forchtner, 2020). So how does Vox do so in a chapter called 'Green Spain'? It does so as follows:

(52)   Spain is a nation of unparalleled beauty, composed of a great diversity of climates and landscapes and rich in natural resources. VOX starts from the principle that the person is the most important element of the environment, so it is necessary to make compatible the care of our natural heritage with the economic development and well-being of Spaniards.

Thus, the environment can be poetically portrayed in the nationalist style of a tourist guide, with which every person and party would agree. Yet, Vox gives it a nationalist-populist twist by changing the focus from nature to Spanish people and their 'well-being'. In sum, nature and the environment do not have priority at the radical right. Indeed, on the same page, Vox already professes its opposition against the 'radical ecologist agenda' of the government (the 'elites' and international organizations), wherever this is inconsistent with the 'well-being' of the Spanish people. Obviously, of all the 'progressive' laws adopted by the socialist government, the law on Climate Change will be rescinded – apparently whatever Spain's international obligations. Of course. Europe (and its 'lobbies') should not tell what Spanish people must do with their land or rural regions, or how much CO_2 it produces.

Given the marginal role of the climate crisis in the electoral programme, very noticeable in very hot and very dry Spain, in Vox's 'green Spain', the general ideology of 'Anti-Environmentalism' (an ideology in need of its own term) need not be further specified by specific Attitudes of a national debate; see also Darian-Smith, 2023). Because of its protection of the 'rural' countryside (and its voters!) any national or international (European) law or rule is violently rejected in this kind of climate Negationism.

Authoritarianism, Militarism

A beloved issue of the radical right is security. Within an authoritarian regime, applying the values of Law-and-Order, crime and hence the police are major topics. The same is true for the combination of (Islamist) terrorism, and hence the military, thus combining militarist and racist ideologies, also to accuse the government of its open-door policy for immigrants.

Theoretically, and different from Militarism, Authoritarianism is not an ideology (corresponding to an ideological group), but a kind of government based on specific values of strict obedience, authority, respect, etc. It is within this conceptual structure that many attitudes can be, and have been, formulated at the radical right, as is the case for various Law and Order issues. Throughout the programme, many policies are formulated in terms of punishment against the laws and rules of the radical right.

As is the case for radical right discourse in Sweden, and as we have seen above, also in Spain immigrants are often associated with crime and violence, whether as potential terrorists or as youth gangs. In such a framework, all policies are in favour of increased finances for the police and protection against criticism of its power abuse. Of course, within the centralist Attitudes of nationalism, autonomous police have no place.

Within Fox's Militarist ideology, Military Academies should be upgraded to universities, and in many ways in the programme Spanish military are celebrated. The programme calls for a 'dignification of the military professional vocation'. And, of course, the ideology of militarism should also be combined with that of racism: The country should be protected by military against the 'invasion' of immigrants.

3.2.2 Vox's Discourse

Compared to the more popular aggressive style of the speeches of Vox politicians, for instance on social media (see, e.g., Pallarés-Navarro & Zugasti, 2022), the 2023 election programme is somewhat more formal and subdued. But it is not a more or less formal statement of ideologies, attitudes, and policies either, as is the case in Chile. Pragmatically it is an attack against the left, and especially Prime Minister Pedro Sánchez, on the one hand, and the independence parties and organizations on the other. Such attacks consist of serial accusations combined with the purported victims of hated policies: *los españoles*, as in the following fragment that opens the programme and might be seen as a short summary of Vox's accusations:

(53) Pedro Sánchez will be remembered as the president who was tough and ruthless with honest Spaniards and soft on criminals, enemies of Spain and foreign elites. His concessions to separatism and his commitment to multilevel Spain has only

> benefited the regional elites and has allowed the consolidation of an unfair model
> that hinders the prosperity and well-being of Spaniards.

Hence, although rhetorically enhanced in many ways, and using hyperbolic qualifications (*tough, ruthless*) and the usual populist ingroup-outgroup polarization (*ruthless* vs. *honest*), abstract words (e.g., *homogenization*) and sentence length complexity bear witness of the formal style of the official election programme. In that sense the programme is different from the more direct style of the parliamentary debate, on the one hand, and the very popular style of Wilders' PVV in the Netherlands, which occasionally is closer to spoken political discourse. Perhaps most characteristic of the lexical style of the programme is the selection of very negative evaluative words, not necessarily typical of a popular spoken style, such as *sinister.*

After these extremely negative opinions on the current government and on regional parties and policies, the second major part of the chapters of the programme are long lists of promises, all in future verb tense – as may be expected of an election programme.

3.2.3 Vox: Conclusions

As is the case in many European countries and the United States, the radical right in Spain can be characterized by an ideological cluster of Nationalism, Racism, Catholicism, Machismo, Neoliberalism, and Militarism at the basis of a large number of attitudes that are at the basis of Vox's public discourse.

In this study, the focus is on ideologies and attitudes, rather than the details of discourse structure. A broader study, also of many other discourse genres of Vox, would need to focus on the specific discourse structures of the radical right, of which in this study we only mentioned the usual populist polarization between Elites and the People, and some obvious aspects of a formal election programme style pragmatically consisting of accusations and promises.

As a final political conclusion of this study, it may be asserted that the ideologies, attitudes, policies and planned bills of Vox in this electoral programme would mean a retrograde of decades of citizen rights and a programme for an illiberal state should Vox come to power. Some of these serious changes have already been implemented in the provinces where Vox joined a government of the Partido Popular.

3.3 The Netherlands: Party for Freedom (PVV)

The Netherlands has an international image of a progressive country, an image carefully construed by the national and international media. It has been only lately that this image has undergone correction by the news about the growing success of radical right parties after 2000. Already in the 1980s there was the anti-immigrant Centrumpartij, which however had only 1 seat in the national parliament of 150 seats, though more in local elections (see Mudde, 2000). In the 1990s, political views on immigration began to radicalize after a lecture of the leader of the conservative party (VVD), Fritz Bolkestein (Van Dijk, 2003). It was Pim Fortuyn, a gay professor at the Erasmus University in Rotterdam, whose anti-immigration and Islamophobic ideas made an impact. In 2002, his new party obtained a third of the seats in the Rotterdam city council. He rejected frequent media comparisons with European radical right politicians such as Jean Marie le Pen and Jörg Haider. Just before the national elections of 2002 he was assassinated, the first political assassination in the Netherlands since 1672.

The real success of the radical right in the Netherlands came in 2006 with the foundation of the Islamophobic radical right *Partij voor de Vrijheid* (PVV, Party for Freedom) by Geert Wilders. It obtained twenty-four seats in parliament in the 2010 general election, the third-largest party, four of twenty seats in the European Parliament in 2014, but had less success in later national and EP elections. In the national elections of 2023, the PVV became the largest political party in the Netherlands, with 37 of 150 seats in parliament, claiming to form a coalition government with Wilders as Prime Minister.

The impressive popularity of Wilders suggests that racist, anti-immigration, and Islamophobic ideas in the 'progressive' Netherlands were as widespread as in other West-European countries. Indeed, already twenty years earlier I had found this in my own research of racist discourse in the Netherlands (see, e.g., Van Dijk, 1984). For studies of PVV discourse and ideology, see, e.g., Burke, Diba & Antonopoulos, 2020; Kopytowska, 2017; Leezenberg, 2015; Verkuyten & Nooitgedagt, 2019; Vossen, 2017).

Specifically interesting is the social psychological discourse study of Verkuyten and Nooitgedacht (2019), who analysed political debates in Dutch parliament between Wilders and other MPs, focusing on 'marginal' and 'mainstream' representations of 'ordinary people', a topic Wilders, and more generally, radical right parties in Europe claim as their specific domain of democratic legitimation.

Crucial in this case is that for Wilders, and again in general for the radical right, their defence of 'ordinary people' is limited to white, autochthonous people, with the characteristic slogan of 'Our own people first', as also was the case in France with Le Pen's slogan 'Les Français d'abord'. Another aspect of such a debate is the question of actual social policies in favour of 'ordinary people', and not a mere discursive strategy to gain votes. Indeed, where analysts may find 'socialist' attitudes in the discourse of the radical right, one conclusion of such analyses may be that this strategy is rather one of pseudo-socialism as a way to compete with real socialism at the Left.

3.3.1 The Electoral Programme of the PVV

The ideology of a one-member party such as the PVV in fact is a reflection of the personal ideas of Wilders, though shared and construed by voters, followers, and international contacts (see, e.g., Rooduijn, 2014b). The programme 2021–2025[3] was a typically populist, Islamophobic text with fragments such as:

(54)   The Islam doesn't belong to the Netherlands. (. . .) And that there is nothing more unwise than to give free rein to the Islamic ideology that wants to take away our freedom. (. . .) Political games, corrupt lawsuits and Islamic fatwas will not stop me. (. . .) Islam is not primarily a religion, but the most violent political ideology in existence. The word Islam means 'submission' and that is exactly what it is aiming for: fighting all non-Muslims, until everything and everyone is Islamic. That is why everywhere in the world where Islam plays a role, there is unfreedom, misery and violence. The freedom and dignity of non-Muslims, dismissed as 'kafrs', is literally and metaphorically violence done. Jews, Christians, gays, apostates, and women are often the first victims of Islamization; unfortunately, we also see this in the Netherlands. It is inexcusable that the political elite of Europe and of the Netherlands has welcomed this terrible Islam with open arms.

The new election programme for the 2023 elections is still Islamophobic, but slightly toned down as we'll see next. The new program of 2023 has 7,755 words (54 pages) of 13 chapters, of which – significantly – the main topic 'Asylum and Immigration' comes first. The other chapters are about economic issues (such as prices and pensions) and a somewhat surprising list of quite heterogeneous topics: Security, Care, Housing Market, Climate and Energy, Farmers, Fishermen and Animals, Democracy, Culture and Public Service Broadcasting, Education, Defence Mobility and Water Management, Foreign Affairs, EU, and Development Aid and Finance.

Interestingly, the Preface of the programme self-identifies its right-wing political-ideological position:

(55)   The PVV opts for social right-wing policy.
Immigration and law and order, but socially on purchasing power and care.

The claim to advocate social policies sometimes are interpreted in the sense that PVV is not just right-wing – and Wilders himself often presents his party as neither Right nor Left. The same Preface summarizes the main points of the programme as follows, which needs to be cited at length:

(56)   After years of demolition policy, our country must be rebuilt. The priorities need to be fundamentally shifted.

---

[3] The 2021–2025 programme of the PVV was analysed in an earlier version of this paper.

No more spending billions on left-liberal ideological policies like nitrogen and climate. No more open borders and unaffordable mass immigration. No more throwing billions abroad.

But investments in and for the Dutch. (. . .)

A stronger and prouder Netherlands.

A country where the Dutch are cherished again.

Because the Netherlands is no longer the Netherlands.

(. . .) Our country is overcrowded. Our neighbourhoods and cities are often unrecognizable with a lot of nuisance and crime. We must reclaim the Netherlands. Closing our borders to even more fortune seekers from other cultures is necessary. And real refugees should no longer be received here, but in their own region.

There must also be an end to discrimination against Dutch people. After all, it is our country. (. . .) our money must also go to our own people. Lower taxes so that, for example, groceries and energy bills become cheaper. But lower rents and fewer excise duties on petrol are also needed. Just like much-needed investments in healthcare, police and education. It is an unprecedented disgrace how elderly care is being dismantled in the Netherlands. Our elderly deserve the best care and a good pension.

We must also take back our national sovereignty. Regain control of our own borders, money and laws. We no longer want dictates from unelected European Commissioners about climate or nitrogen, about farmers' hatred, or letting asylum seekers in. We choose the Dutch interest. And zero more Dutch euros go to Brussels, Italy, Africa or any redistribution fund. We would like to cooperate intensively with other countries, but not in a political union like the EU.

There is also no place in the Netherlands for sympathizers of violent jihad and Sharia. The Netherlands is not an Islamic country. Our own culture and secular laws always take precedence and if you don't like it, you leave.

We want a safe, strong and sovereign Netherlands.

A self-confident Netherlands where we always put our own population in 1st place with our heads held high.

That is my Netherlands.

These points of the programme already imply the following ideologies to be examined in more detail next: Nationalism, Racism (Islamophobia), Anti-Ecologism and Neoliberalism.

Racism

As has been made explicit in the Preface, the dominating ideology is the Nativist cluster of Nationalism and Racism. This means that most nationalist topics have a racist dimension, and most racist topics are related to nationalism. This is how the programme begins after the Preface:

(57)   Our beautiful Netherlands has been severely degraded by the constant asylum tsunami and mass immigration. (. . .) And that while the Netherlands is overpopu-lated. (. . .) It is incomprehensible that virtually all political parties have saddled us

with insane open-borders policies. Because there is no part of our society that is not affected by the admission of so many fortune seekers. Our culture, and Western way of life, is threatened by the entry of large numbers of people, often from non-Western, Islamic countries. Even Syrian terrorists enter our country undisturbed with the influx of asylum seekers. On average, people with a non-western foreign background are on average 3 times more likely to be suspected of a crime than native Dutch people. (...) Our welfare state is under great pressure from non-western foreigners who benefit massively from our benefits and other provisions. More than half of the income support recipients in the Netherlands now have a non-western foreign background.

Election programmes are supposed to formulate the (partisan) definition of the major problems of society. For the PVV and Wilders this is obviously first of all the presence of immigrants. The selective focus is repeatedly on 'non-Western' immigrants, which shows that the attitude is not just general xenophobia, but (cultural) racism, because they are seen as a threat to 'our culture and Western way of life'. This sociopolitical definition of the situation is rhetorically enhanced with the usual flow and disaster metaphors (*asylum tsunami, influx*), the numbers game (*overpopulated; so many; large numbers; 3 times more, more than half*), gradation adverbs (*massively*) and negative descriptions of immigrants and refugees (*fortune seekers*). As is typically the case of most of the paragraphs of the programme, the racist focus on immigration is at the same time associated with Security attitudes about crime and terrorism, typically associated with Arabs, and with the attitude of Welfare Chauvinism defining the alleged priority of social benefits. As argued earlier, ideological debate, even in this kind of sociopolitical party programmes, is not at the level of general ideologies, but about attitudes about issues made prominent precisely by (Radical) Right parties; overpopulation, terrorism, benefits, our way of life. The rest of this first chapter lists the many other ways immigration is alleged to have negative influence on the country: education, health care and of course the economy: 'Every year it costs the Dutch taxpayer 24 billion euros', a number game associated with the populist figure of the 'taxpayer'.

Example (57) testifies to a crucial further issue. Both in the national and the international media, a point is made that Wilders and the PVV in the 2023 programme had become less radically Islamophobic, such as abandoning the policy of closing mosques. Such a change of policy would be a condition to form a coalition with other conservative parties. What has been overlooked in such commentary, as well as in the ongoing negotiations to form a government, is that the programme is hardly less racist, as is made explicit in the cultural supremacy elements of example 57. Although no doubt it is true that not all people voting for the PVV are racist, it remains true that voting for, and governing with, an explicitly racist party hardly is consistent with democratic values, but rather reveals an attitude for which racism is not a major moral, social, or political problem. It is in this sense that the traditional image of the Netherlands as a progressive country is hardly true for a very large part of its citizens and politicians in 2023.

Us vs. Them

A common *topos* of racist programmes, policies, and discourse is the alleged inequality of the distribution of services and money between Us and Them, a standard argument we often encountered in our analysis of immigration debates in the UK (van Dijk, 1993):

(58) It is absurd that Dutch politics has increasingly considered the well-being of asylum seekers and other immigrants to be more important than the well-being and prosperity of the Dutch. Asylum seekers feast on free delicious buffets on luxury cruise ships, while Dutch families have to cut back on groceries. Health care that has become unaffordable for many Dutch people is provided free of charge to asylum seekers. And by pampering illegal immigrants, Dutch people even have to pay for people who are not even allowed to be here.

Such standard arguments in this case are associated with the populist topos of the alleged poverty of 'Dutch families', reinforcing the racist polarization between Us vs. Them. In this way, not only the programme construes a racist picture of immigrants and refugees, but at the same time introduces the social issue of cutbacks, allowing the obvious inference that economic problems of ordinary people are largely due to immigration. In other words, the programme does not misinform about the social situation but at the same shows how to think about it.

The ideologically based Us vs. Them topos not only defines the issue of immigration but appears throughout the programme. Thus, in the Economy chapter, this topic of the allegedly unfair consequences for Dutch people is reformulated as follows, with the usual rhetoric of the numbers game, and as sequence of 'foreignness' (*Africa, Brussels*):

(59) Billions go to a war that is not ours, billions to Africa, billions to Brussels, billions to nonsensical climate and nitrogen policies, billions to mass immigration. Our welfare state is being drained by non-Western profiteers, for whom everything is arranged down to the last detail. Meanwhile, the Dutch are forced to skip meals; in 2023, the Red Cross will even distribute food parcels in the Netherlands. That is downright absurd.

Asylum

This very negative description of the social situation in the Netherlands ('discrimination against Dutch people'), attributed to immigrants obviously requires policies announced by the PVV such as an 'asylum freeze'. Such a stop of poor refugees must of course be argued – in terms of the cultural topos of rich Arabs:

(60)   And real refugees can be accommodated in safe countries in their own region. Wealthy countries such as Kuwait, the United Arab Emirates, or Saudi Arabia do not have to do anything now, because the residence permits in the Netherlands are up for grabs. In addition to stemming the influx, the outflow of migrants must be increased. Illegal immigrants must be detained And criminals are – if necessary after denaturalisation – forcibly deported from our country.

Without detailed further argument for these policies, the programme casually mentions the usual attitude of Sending Immigrants Back, and the security issue of 'illegal immigration' and 'criminal immigrants'. Indeed, these are topics that, also in the Netherlands, have been discussed since decades in public and party discourse about immigration. Hence, they can only be mentioned briefly because such policies are simply presupposed – and not only by the radical right. The conclusion of such policies – and hence the reason to vote for the PVV is clear, and argued in terms of the topos of commonsense argumentation:

(61)   The PVV allows common sense to prevail again on the failing immigration policy. We have the best ideas for this, such as a total asylum freeze. Because the Netherlands is packed. We have previously called for an opt-out from EU regulations, the criminalisation of illegality and the reintroduction of national border control. On the way to the asylum freeze that we envisage and necessary, we support measures that will significantly reduce the influx of asylum seekers and other migrants. In short, we are going to do everything we can to stop the disruptive asylum and immigration disaster! And with the restriction of the asylum and migration influx to the Netherlands, the Islamization of our country will also be significantly limited!

The end of the chapter on immigration reminds the readers (and the voters) that the problem of Wilders's is not just ('massive') immigration, as elsewhere in Europe, but especially the main issue of 'Islamization'.

International Aid

The Nativist combination of Racism and Nationalism also applies to the attitude on international aid. Whereas Wilders is proud of Dutch history, colonialism, and the military, no such pride can be found about development aid. On the contrary, the slogan is 'Our Own Country First', of course combined with the negative representation of refugees, apparently not only of Muslims:

(62)   The population of Africa is growing this century to more than 4 billion inhabitants and is doomed to poverty and war by corrupt ruling classes. The tsunami of fortune seekers to Europe, which is already present, will therefore only increase further.

However, Islamophobia also dominates in this chapter, because international aid and cooperation obviously is withdrawn from countries where the sharia is practised:

(63)   Relations with Islamic countries that adhere to Sharia law and from which, moreover, Dutch parliamentarians are threatened with death without these countries taking action against it, will be immediately severed.

However, in the Netherlands Islamophobia may be combined with attitudes that are based on feminist values of gender identity, showing again how ideologies and attitudes are adapted to the sociopolitical context:

(64)   The Netherlands is reducing its diplomatic presence in the countries that have signed the Cairo Declaration on Human Rights, which subordinates all rights and freedoms to Sharia law, which, among other things, restricts freedom of expression and makes gender inequality a starting point.

Nationalism obviously is inconsistent with internationalism and globalism, a well-known feature of the radical right. Although elsewhere at the radical right in Europe the hardly attractive example of Brexit has reduced usual opposition against the European Union, Wilders maintains his distance, and even proposes a Nexit unlikely to be widely supported in the Netherlands:

(65)   The Party for Freedom opts for a sovereign Netherlands. A Netherlands that is once again in charge of its own money, its own borders and makes its own rules. As a sovereign country, we strive for strong bilateral and economic ties with other countries. This intensive cooperation between countries does not require political union, such as the EU, an institution that is increasingly seizing power, eating up taxpayers' money and imposing diktats on us. The PVV wants a binding referendum on Nexit.

The crucial ideological value is sovereignty, repeated twice.

Nationalism

As we have argued earlier, many of the reasons of the emergence of the radical right is its illiberal reaction against influence of the fundamental liberal changes since the 1960s. The problem for a RR party in the Netherlands is that many of the results of this 'liberal revolution' have become consensual among large parts of the population, as is the case for abortion, euthanasia, and gay marriage. Hence, an RR programme can hardly expect to stimulate many voters against such liberal changes in society. Indeed, only Dutch and European racism is not challenged by dominant antiracism, so that many racist attitudes may find an expression in most RR programmes in Europe, as well as in the Netherlands.

Hence, within a populist argument, on at least some topics, liberal policies may be criticized:

(66) Our democracy is not working. Time and again, the same group of people gets their way: highly educated Netherlands. It is overwhelmingly oriented towards D66 and GroenLinks and other left-liberals. All with the same ideas about the EU, mass immigration and climate. That is why our sovereignty is being given away to Brussels, our country is being filled with windmills and the Netherlands is full of asylum seekers' centres. The rest are allowed to pay taxes, but not to participate. The elite rules.

The populist argument is interesting in order to show that it is not simply a polarization between the elites and 'the rest', but a very specific elites, repeated several times in the chapter on Democracy Culture and Broadcasting: those who vote for parties on the Left. In other words, the programme in a few words summarizes the participants of the culture war. At the same time, the Others are not only the higher educated at the Left, but also Brussels and hence the EU as the typical enemy of the Right.

Within the combined cluster of Nationalism and Racism, various topics of history and colonialism are examined in this chapter about culture:

(67) The PVV loves the Netherlands. We are proud of our culture, identity and traditions. We must therefore retain them. Not erase them. The left-wing hatred in which heroes of our history are reviled is ending. The apologies for the history of slavery and the police actions, as done by the King, are withdrawn. Zwarte Piet remains.

In a few lines, the programme summarizes various topics of its nationalist attitudes, typically associated with pride, and implying revisionist attitudes about slavery and colonial oppression in Indonesia (typically mitigated with the usual euphemism of 'police actions'). If liberal action, such as national excuses for slavery, is engaged in by the King, the typical RR admiration for royalty (as is the case in Spain) is obviously cancelled. And the Nativist cluster of Racism and Nationalism is also applied in the very brief reference to blackface 'Zwarte Piet' (Van Dijk, 1988), a traditional figure of the children feast of Sinterklaas, which has become increasingly controversial during the last years.

Topics of nativist discrimination are reversed by the usual topos of discrimination reversal we also frequently encountered in interviews with Dutch citizens talking about immigration, many years before the success of RR parties (Van Dijk, 1984):

(68) Native Dutch people are not protected. They are disadvantaged and discriminated against. In politics, in art, in public broadcasting, in science and in many

municipalities. They call this 'preferential policy' or 'positive discrimination'. That is coming to an end.

Education

As we have seen in Spain, part of the RR culture war are the reactionary concerns about education, where liberal progress on racism and sexuality is attacked in terms of anti-woke measures, especially in the United States and the UK (Cammaerts, 2022). Such would in principle be less the case in liberal views that have become consensus in the Netherlands. So, here Wilders needs to tread with care, although he already has declared highly educated progressives as the enemy elite. Obviously, the quality of education should be a concern of all political parties:

(69) Education has fallen into free fall under [PM] Rutte's cabinets. A quarter of our pupils are semi-illiterate and in some neighbourhoods more than half of the children no longer reach the required reading level. This means that 25% of our students are sent semi-illiterate into this complicated society. They will have the greatest difficulty in coping for the rest of their lives, unable to fully develop. That is a disgrace of the first order for a developed country like the Netherlands. There is also a huge shortage of teachers, because fewer and fewer people want to stand in front of the classroom. As a result, many schools have been forced to switch to a four-day teaching week.

Such a negative description is formulated with rhetorical devices such as metaphors (*free fall*) and the usual numbers game. To state the problem in this fragment already suggests the solution, and indeed the next paragraph reads:

(70) In addition, the massive influx of asylum seekers means that our basic education system is also under serious pressure. In a city like The Hague, no less than four classes are added per month! Totally unsustainable and uncomfortable given the ever-declining educational performance.

Thus, as a major issue of the culture war, education is also associated with the topic of immigration, and hence with a racist ideology. The rest of the Education chapters is directed against educational renewal and wants traditional teaching. But of course, the main RR accusation of liberal education is indoctrination, as we also have seen in Spain:

(71) We are seeing an increase in political indoctrination in schools. School children are indoctrinated with climate activism, gender madness, and with a sense of shame about our country's history. We want education that is free of political activism. We want politically neutral teachers in the classroom and politically neutral textbooks in the classroom.

As this example shows, RR party discourse combines various ideologies and attitudes in complex hate objects, as is the case for liberal teaching, featuring anti-ecologism (*climate activism*), sexism (*gender madness*) and nationalist revisionism (*shame about our country's history*). However, in the Netherlands this means an uneasy combination of a liberal consensus, e.g., about the identity of women and men and LGTB+, on the one hand, and the racist attitude of Islamophobia:

(72)   We want to preserve special education and Article 23 of the Constitution. Freedom of education is a great asset. However, there is no place for education that is at odds with the main principles on which our society is based: freedom, equality between men and women, heterosexual or LGBTI, religious or religious leaver. This means that we do not give Islamic education a place in our system and therefore ban it.

Militarism

Traditionally, the radical right is not exactly pacifist (Mudde, 2000). And indeed, also Wilders celebrates the military, and does so with enthusiastic rhetoric:

(73)   The PVV is proud of our Defence, of our soldiers and of our veterans! The Dutch Armed Forces are a wonderful part of Dutch history. The successes of our navy have captured the imagination for centuries. We are not going to go along with erasing that beautiful history. Nor do we go along with criticizing our Indian veterans. These are heroes that we should cherish, because they have worked in good conscience for our country under difficult circumstances.

As is the case for many paragraphs in the programme, also here several ideologies are expressed at the same time: militarism and nationalism, such as the characteristic revisionism of (violent) colonial history. The denial (*we are not going ...*) presupposes that his revisionism challenges the recent liberal tendency to make excuses for past human rights violations, as the Dutch King had recently done. The 2023 programme at the same time comments on the current situation criticizing military aid for Ukraine 'since we can't even defend our own country'. And, as may be expected, this statement perfectly well combines with the racist attitudes on immigration and security (*street terror*):

(74)   What we do need to do is use our Defense for national security. So for the defense of our own territory. For the PVV, this also includes defending against the asylum rush on our country. As in the pre-Schengen era, we must use defence for border control. Then we can prevent asylum seekers from setting foot on Dutch soil. And where the police in the Netherlands can no longer cope

with large-scale street terror, our people from the Royal Netherlands
Marechaussee can help to keep the Dutch streets safe.

Security

As we'll see next in the radical right programme of the Sweden Democrats,
Security issues are a prominent topic of the PVV programme, often associated
with authoritarian attitudes about Law and order. The semantic strategy of the
PVV programme is to polarize negative topics of criminal threat with the beauty
of relaxed life in the neighbourhood:

(75) For the PVV, safety is and remains a top priority. We find it appalling that security
in our country has become far from self-evident. Where criminality used to be an
incident, millions of Dutch people are now victims of crime every year. Cozy
working-class neighbourhoods have been transformed into no-go areas, where
street terrorists rule. (...) Stabbings and shootings alternate at a rapid pace,
conductors are no longer sure of their lives on the train, and a beautiful
sunny day at the beach is spoiled by Moroccan riot youths in particular.

And, as is the case in Sweden, also here crime is typically attributed to immigrant youth, a well-known attitude dominated by Racism.

As may be expected, such a situation requires the usual Law and Order
policies: thousands of extra police officers, long prison sentences, election of
police commissioners, and harsh prison life.

Again, since any negative topic must be attributed to immigrants, or at least
associated with (Arab) Others, the programme states that there are thousands of
sympathizers of the Jihad.

Social Policies

Although large parts of the programme associate social problems with immigration, this is not consistent in the PVV programme, which self-identifies by
being ideologically ambiguous, and even called 'social' by researchers (Vossen,
2017). Thus, the chapter on Care is formulated in empathic terms, for instance in
paragraphs such as:

(76) Our care is invaluable and at the same time unaffordable for more and more
people. They can no longer pick up the medicines prescribed by their doctor at
the pharmacy, because they can no longer pay the deductible or because the
medicines are no longer reimbursed. As a result, their health deteriorates faster
and they are more likely to become more expensive patients. (...) More and
more emergency departments and intensive care units are being closed. Due to
competition, more and more care is disappearing from regional hospitals and
more and more are falling over. (...) Then there is no ambulance brother who
comes when the need arises, no nutrition consultant who brings food around the

hospital and no one who comes home to help clean if you are too old and too difficult to walk to do it yourself. Then there is no doctor who takes away your worries or sends you on, and no more brilliant specialist who cures you.

Similar passages can be found in the chapter on Housing, although in that case lack of housing may be attributed to immigration, whereas in other passages it is claimed that some categories of immigrants get priority.

(77) The borders are wide open, and everyone who enters wants housing. Of all the homes that will be built in the coming years, no less than 75% are intended for migrants. That's complete madness. The open borders policy and the enormous population growth are simply impossible to build against!

Climate Crisis

Radical right ideologies and attitudes are known to be anti-environmental, and the climate crisis is typically denied or mitigated. In a country that prides itself of its progressive policies and respect for scientific research, how does the PVV take a stand on one of the most important issues of international debate and policies? Wilders prefers denial with well-known commonsense fallacies:

(78) For decades, we have been frightened by climate change. Although the predicted disaster scenarios – about the world that would perish – became increasingly extreme over the years, none of them ever materialized. (. . .) The climate has been changing for centuries. We adapt to changing circumstances. We do this through sensible water management, by raising the dikes when necessary and by providing space for the river. But we stop the hysterical reduction of CO2, with which we as a small country mistakenly think we can 'save' the climate. The Netherlands is responsible for less than half a percent of total global CO2 emissions.

Part of this denial of the environmental situation is a long list of policies PVV will rescind or not implement, such as the closing coalmines and gas pits, construing ('abominable') wind turbines, and construing electric cars. Such descriptions only make sense in a programme if they are relevant for 'ordinary people. Hence the universal threat of higher energy bills, attributed to higher taxes due to environmental policies.

A major topic in the Netherlands are the policies to reduce nitrogen emissions due to extensive farming. Hence, as part of its environmental denials, the PVV defends farmers as potential voters. Indeed, this was one of the reasons a special Farmers Party (the BBB) has recently been grounded. Similar policies are advocated for fishers. Wilders also empathically defends the well-being for animals – most likely also thinking of all those voters who have pets.

Mobility

A special chapter is dedicated to mobility. Part of the general ideology of the denial of the climate crisis, as is the case in Spain and Sweden, is the defence of the holy car:

(79)   For the PVV, mobility is an important condition for freedom and prosperity. We believe that everyone should decide for themselves how someone travels to his or her destination. The government should not interfere.

Examples like this explicitly show the internal structures of ideology: the important role of a general value (freedom) as an argument, as is the case for many forms of RR denial. At the same time such examples show the implementation of the value of individual freedom of neoliberalism in terms of the opposition against government policies. An interesting detail is that in this example the gender inclusive possessive pronouns (*his or her*) are used, different from male chauvinist language use of Vox in Spain – showing the differences of the sociopolitical contexts in formulation of RR discourse in these countries. Consistent with the neoliberal defence of individual car driving, the same chapter also rejects any limitation on flying.

3.3.2 PVV Discourse

Another striking difference with the 2021 programme is not just the less aggressive islamophobia, but especially the much less 'popular' style, often called 'populist'. The programme is still much less formal than those in Chile, Spain, and Sweden, but it seems that Wilders aims at a style level that is no longer the one of the linguistic uses of the street fighter, typical of the unique lexical choices and constructions of the 2021–2015 programme. The 'orality' of the style is especially expressed in frequent, slogan-like short sentences (e.g., *This Must Stop*), the repeated forms of negative appraisal: *absurd, insane, hysterical, hideous*, etc., the frequent metaphors (*asylum tsunami*) and the rhetorical number game (*millions, billions*), popular compound verbs (e.g., *take back*), and a large number of nominal compounds in Dutch where English or Spanish would have separate words (e.g., *asylum-inflow*). This popular style of the PVV and Wilders requires a detailed sociolinguistic analysis, also as a characteristic of RR discourse, which in Chile and Spain would rather characterize parliamentary debates and speeches of politicians.

3.3.3 PVV: Conclusions

Compared to the 2021–2015 programme, the 2023 election programme has toned down especially its rabiate Islamophobic aggression, but there is little doubt about this form of racism, typically associated with youth crime ('street terror'), gender inequality, sharia, jihad, and cultural influence in education and other areas. Such hate speech is usually formulated in terms of the defence of a special interpretation of 'western' values, such as gender equality. But the more general opposition against all 'non-western' immigrants shows that the dominating ideological cluster is the Nativist combination of Racism and Nationalism – as elsewhere in Europe.

The same is true for the various attitudes based on Nationalism in all domains of Dutch society. One might assume that, compared to other countries such as the United States, there is no strong nationalism in the Netherlands in the sense of being proud of national symbols such as the flag, but Wilders's programme shows and presupposes that national pride is ubiquitous, for instance, in the support for the army, glorious Dutch history and its heroes, the countryside, and the revisionist denial of the horrors of Dutch colonial history and slavery. Throughout, the ideological opponents are the representatives of liberal progressivism, as is the case in education and textbooks. Teachers for the PVV must be 'neutral'.

Whereas ethnically non-western immigrants are the THEM of racist polarization, the 'populist' opponent (the elites) of Wilders and the PVV is the highly educated liberal left – showing that there is no general opposition between ordinary people and the power elites in general, but a very specific political one defining the position of the PVV, both against mainstream parties, and specifically against the left, as is the case in Spain.

The other characteristics of the RR discourse of PVV are as may be expected: Climate Crisis denial, anti-internationalism, and anti-EU, Militarism, Law and Order Security and Authoritarianism.

The sociopolitical context influences the main difference with RR ideologies in Chile and Spain: The programme does not even mention such social issues as abortion, euthanasia, or gay marriage, and gender equality is explicitly asserted, though as positive self-presentation against negative characterization of 'backward' Islam and Muslims.

No doubt the PVV is neoliberal, but Wilders knows that apart from racist and nationalist topics, only explicit social issues are able to attract voters, and hence the programme generously formulates many forms of social and financial assistance, for instance of pensioners – and of course of the police.

3.4 Sweden: Sverigedemokrater

Despite the progressive international reputation of Sweden, the Sverigedemokrater (SD) party surprised both Sweden and the rest of the world in 2022 by becoming the largest conservative party in parliament with 20.6 per cent of the vote. Founded in 1988, initially with members of fascist and white nationalist groups, its policies have always been against immigration. In the 2014 election it had 5.7 per cent of the national, and 9.6 per cent of the European vote, 12.9 per cent in the national vote of 2014, and 17.5 per cent in the 2018 election. In 2022 it formed a group with the Moderates, Christian Democrats, and the Liberals. Its 2022 election campaign features complete rejection of refugees, stricter policies on work permits, and a tougher stance on gang violence. Its official ideology is 'democratic nationalism' and a focus on Law and Order. Our ideological analysis is based on its 2022 Election Platform.

3.4.1 The Electoral Programme of the Sweden Democrats

Compared to the programmes of radical right parties in Spain and the Netherlands, the programme of Sverigedemokrater is of considerable length (36 chapters, 61 pages, and more than 20,000 words). As may be expected, the first chapters show its main issues: Crime and Punishment (specifically also on Gang Crime and Victims of Crime), Police, Terrorism, Integration and Migration (including honour crimes), and Equality. The rest of the programme is about the usual other social domains, such as the Economy, Jobs, (small) business, the Environment, Climate and Energy, the Countryside, the Labour market, Childcare and School and Education, Youth and the Elderly, Family, and Health Care, but also less common topics such as Public Waste, the Car, Hunting, Agriculture and Forestry, and Animal Welfare. Here are some fragments of the Introduction that provide a summary of the general ideological orientation of the programme and the party:

(80)   For a long time, Swedish politics has been about putting interests other than those of Sweden and its citizens first. (...) The insecurity, which has grown into a structural social problem, is the most serious consequence of the borderless migration policy pursued by a long series of governments. Recreating a society governed by the rule of law to rely on will be a thematically central task when the Sweden Democrats gain governing influence. (...) Swedish society and culture is basically something to be proud of. Few countries have historically been able to match the Swedes' ability to combine individual freedom with great care for each other. Previous generations of Swedes have built up a society that for a long time was among the foremost in the world. But gradually progressive progress has shifted to tolerance to the intolerant.

The topic of 'own (Swedish) citizens first' is common to all radical right parties, and so is the ideological based attitude of migration as the main cause of any other problem, including Law and Order – all dominated by a Racism ideology and the ideological norm of strict governance (see, e.g., Bolin, Liden & Nyhlen,

2014). The topic of Pride of the country (as the best in the world) is characteristic of a nationalist ideology, also very prominent in the PVV programme in the Netherlands. Typical is also the nostalgia of the past – when all was better than now (see Elgenius & Rydgren, 2017, 2019).

Even more than most radical right parties, the programme focuses first and foremost on many aspects of Crime and its consequences. As is the case in the Netherlands, this and many other issues are related and explained in terms of migration:

(81) Restoring security for citizens must be an overarching thematic mission of the next government. In recent decades, insecurity has spread across Sweden and fundamentally changed the social climate. The link to harmful and excessive immigration over a long period of time is obvious.

Within the overall norm of Law and Order, all crimes should be punished harshly, and foreign criminals should be deported – a general topic of radical right parties in Europe. Specific for the Swedish programme is the attention for 'gang crime', also associated with immigrants, and rhetorically emphasized as a threat to 'innocent and ordinary people' as victims – a topic of a special chapter of the programme:

(82) A new brutal gang culture has hit Sweden as a result of the immigration policy pursued by both nonsocialist and social democratic governments. The number of segregated areas where gangs and clans have pushed back Swedish society has grown in both number and in the degree of segregation. Shootings, blasts and robberies have become commonplace from north to south and are increasingly affecting the lives of innocent and ordinary people.

Of course, such an analysis also requires special attention for the police and the judiciary, which obviously must be increased and better paid.

In the same perspective also the topic of (especially Islamist) terrorism is associated with immigration and multiculturalism:

(83) Terrorism and extremism are the ultimate expression of the failed multiculturalism project conducted in Sweden. In our country, terrorists and extremists should neither be allowed to exist nor be nurtured. The security and cohesion of society must be safeguarded. Terrorism as a phenomenon has recently grown stronger in Sweden and Europe, several terrorist acts have taken place and everyone remembers the attack on Drottninggatan in Stockholm, where several people including a young girl tragically lost their lives. At the same time, we know that Islamist extremism is financed both through state funds and foreign donations. Hundreds of people have travelled from Sweden to fight for IS, and many have returned. Security threats in the form of terrorist imams are allowed to remain in Sweden even without citizenship, because they risk being exposed in their home countries.

Prominent Extremist Right (e.g., neo-Nazi) violence and terrorism (especially also in Sweden) obviously are not topicalized (Ravndal, 2018). Hence, the Law and Order topic in radical right discourse is not applied to Our Own People, and hence also controlled by Nativism.

As may be expected, the topic of integration, also related to migration, emphasizes that immigrants must adapt and hence learn Swedish. Using a euphemism for 'sending back' the programme says, 'People who do not learn Swedish, do not want to work and do not want to adapt to our norms and values should be helped to return home.' Also in this perspective, the topic of migration in general is introduced as follows:

(84)   Sweden needs to turn decades of irresponsible mass immigration into focusing on voluntary return activities. Asylum immigration from countries outside our immediate area must stop and more people who are in Sweden without the right or who have no connection to Swedish society should leave in the future than who immigrate to Sweden.

Interestingly, and different from radical right discourse in other countries, immigration and asylum are accepted for people 'from neighbouring countries (probably within a more general ideological unity of Nordic peoples; see also Hutton, 2017). In the same perspective of associating migrants with negative issues is the topic of 'honour', only discussed in the Swedish RR programme, found to be incompatible with 'Swedish Culture' and focusing on parental control of girls, veils, and femicide (see Björktomta, 2019).

It is not surprising that the chapter on equality, on the one hand, celebrates advanced gender equality in Sweden, but then focuses on the increasing limitations of the freedoms of immigrant women (see also Askola, 2019). Indeed, this is how radical right ideological bias controls any political topic: in this case combining progressive gender equality with attitudes controlled by racist ideology (see also De Lange & Mudde, 2015; Dietze & Roth, 2020; Kottig, 2016). Within such a nativist controlled programme, and despite the feminist consensus in Sweden, there is, of course, no attention for the many forms of sexual harassment by Swedish men. Most nationalist discourse ignores the many forms of deviance or crime of 'our own people' – as well as their history, as is the case for revisionism about slavery and colonialism in the Netherlands and Spain, and past dictatorship, as is the case in Spain.

In the chapter on the economy, the programmes states:

(85)   The Sweden Democrats are neither a right-wing party nor a left-wing party. On the contrary, we agree on the realization that strong growth, conditions for business and entrepreneurship, and policies that stimulate people to work and

strive are a prerequisite for being able to rebuild a welfare that can provide security for all citizens.

This declaration of 'economic neutrality' is not uncommon of radical right parties, but in this case it might only be correct for the domain of the economy. No doubt Sweden has an economy controlled by neoliberal principles, but at the same time it has exceptional welfare provisions. The preference for Swedish companies and citizens also means reducing the costs of EU migration policies and climate action. More specific is the chapter on small business:

(86) Businesses create jobs, growth and a vibrant local community. But running a business is usually associated with great efforts and risks as well as a often inhumane workload and stress. Bureaucracy, regulatory burden, taxes and admin-istrative costs risk taking the focus away from the core business and taking the edge off an entrepreneur's driving force. Despite long-standing ambitions to reduce regulatory hassle, studies show that the burden over time has remained at high levels or increased. Unnecessarily strict conditions in industry standards and in procurements often make it difficult for smaller players to enter the market.

This passage shows a clear focus on the value of 'liberty' of neoliberal ideolo-gies, including a rejection of rules, taxes, and 'strict conditions' and hence government control.

The other chapters and topics of the election programme of Sweden Democrats are less marked by typical radical right ideology and attitudes, for instance in the chapter on the environment, featuring such topics as biodiversity, forestry, and the toxic waters of the Baltic sea, all to be managed by policies based on research.

On the other hand, the chapter on climate hardly recommends changes of policy, because 'While this creates concern, there are great reasons to be confident about man's ability to innovate to manage and combat climate change', implying less concern, while emphasizing, as does the PVV pro-gramme for the Netherlands, that Sweden only accounts for a few percent of the world's emissions. Indeed, environmental policies should not diminish Swedish competitiveness, as may be expected from an attitude also controlled by a neoliberal ideology. In the same perspective, energy problems should be resolved by nuclear plants.

As is briefly the case for the programme of VOX, the programme of the Sweden Democrats pays extensive attention to all issues related to the country-side (presumably distinct from the 'leftist' cities), where Swedish people live and work (not where 'the big city dwellers to have somewhere to stay on holiday'), such as the promotion of local small businesses and reducing the price of gasoline for people who need their car, rural roads, or who need to fly in the large country, and policies of agriculture, forestry and animal protection. Hence also a special chapter on the car, and the protection of hunting (e.g., against the EU policies on arms).

Also within a neoliberal ideology is the combination of job security and business 'flexibility and growth', as part of the strong social-democratic tradition of Sweden ('Swedish model'). The same is true for benefits and unemployment policies. Within such a consensus, the programme does not even limit benefits to 'own people', a form of welfare chauvinism typical of PVV policies in the Netherlands.

Of course, positive housing policies are always relevant, since also in Sweden young people have difficulties finding an apartment. Despite the limitations for 'big city dwellers' in the countryside, policies are propagated for building houses in nice surroundings such as beaches – indeed there may also be voters among these citizens.

Finally, more explicitly ideologically influenced are family topics such as childcare, in which obviously progressive ideas on gender are not espoused, despite their influence in the country:

(87)   Gender pedagogy as it stands today should not be used as it is largely focused on blurring gender differences. All children should have the right to be who they are. Swedish childcare has previously been seen as an example in large parts of the world, a position we intend to regain.

In other words, gay and trans children don't need to know 'who they are'. The overall ideology of the country may be progressive, but radical right norms and values of patriarchy need at least to be mentioned in the programme, also as part of the chapter on youth. And within the ideologies of Racism and Nationalism, as is the case of the radical right in Spain and the Netherlands, also the Sweden Democrats obviously limit teaching of immigrant children in Swedish only. This is more generally the case for education, of course also plagued by (Islamist) immigration:

(88)   Few sectors have been hit as hard by failed integration policies and excessive immigration as schools. The results have fallen and it is all too common for the school environment to be characterized by insecurity, disorder and substandard pedagogy. (. . .) With the goal of counteracting segregation and extremist influence of school students, we want measures to be taken for this type of school to be banned, for example, Islamist.

As may be expected of an RR-programme, special care is dedicated not only to families ('the basic community of society') and children but also to the elderly and their pensions. Within the chapter on equality, abortion is a right that is guaranteed, and hence very different from the adherence to family values of radical right parties in Catholic countries such as Chile. Within the framework of nativist policies, also international aid, one of the most extensive of the world, is hardly propagated, casually combined with a reminder of the Law-and-Order perspective and the prevailing anti-immigration attitude:

(89)   Therefore, the Sweden Democrats want to see effective aid that goes to those most in need of help and that does not feed corruption or terrorism. („„) Sweden pays more in development assistance than any other country. More of the Swedes' tax money goes every year to international aid than to the Swedish police, prosecution and judicial systems combined (...) The interest in creating conditions for persons to return to their home country after a conflict or disaster has ended shall also be taken into account in international assistance.

Similarly, and finally, a strong defence is propagated within the overall nationalist ideology, as a typical Attitude based on an ideology of Militarism.

3.4.2 Sverigedemokrater: Conclusions

The election programme of the Sverigedemokrater shows some of the general ideological perspectives of most radical right parties, primarily the racist attitudes on all topics related immigration, refugees, and Islam, often combined with nationalist issues.

Within the larger sociopolitical consensus in Sweden, many social and family issues are different from those in countries with strong religious and Catholic beliefs, e.g., on abortion. But still, also in Sweden, in this programme we find a moderate form of anti-gender attitudes. Social programmes for the elderly and the unemployed are consistent with the social-democratic consensus, though with a stronger neoliberal influence, e.g., in the protection of (Swedish) business competitiveness. Though marginally present in Spain and the Netherlands, the radical right programme in Sweden pays extensive attention to the countryside and its people, forestry, hunting, the use of cars, and the environment.

As may have been obvious of the quoted fragments, the style of the programme is formal and programmatic, and – except from some topics – hardly populist in the sense of very hyperbolic word selection, exaggerated accusations, strong ingroup-outgroup polarization – except the negative representation of migrants, refugees and especially gangs, and hence the prominent Law and Order topic.

4 Conclusions

The theoretical and analytical findings of this study may be summarized by the following conclusions.

4.1 Theory of Ideology

Studies of radical right ideologies must be based on a detailed, multidisciplinary theory of ideologies, ideology clusters, and the more specific socially shared attitudes, as forms of social cognition, related to personal opinions and emotions of the mental models of individual members of ideological groups and their social practices, especially discourse. Although studies of radical right parties in political science do refer to ideologies, these studies do not provide or refer to theories of ideology in terms of social cognition, their systematic relations to a theory of attitudes, and the relationship these forms of social cognition and the structures of discourse. This also implies that there is no empirical method to derive ideologies from discourses such as election programmes as studied here.

4.2 The Cultural Backlash of RR-parties

The ideologies of contemporary radical right parties can be partly explained as a reactionary backlash against the cultural revolution since the 1960s defining the profound social changes (mostly but not exclusively) in Europe and the Americas in the fields of the nation, race, gender, sexuality, etc. in favour of the rights of various kinds of minorities. We have seen in the election programmes, and most clearly so in the programme of Vox, that practically all their programmatic elements consist of reactions against liberal values and progressive politics in general, and the current social democratic governments. This is less explicit in the Netherlands and Sweden, where many liberal attitudes (e.g., on abortion) have become part of the dominant cultural consensus, so that in these countries, radical right parties mostly focus on racist and nationalist attitudes, such as immigration or alleged violence of immigrants.

4.3 Populism Is Discursive

The radical right should primarily be characterized in terms of its *political position*, that is, as a radical opposition against other political parties (especially at the left) and their *political* power, and not in ideological terms. Such a position should not be confused with People vs. Elite populism, which is a specific strategy of political discourse (see further). In left-wing political discourse such an opposition is ideologically based, e.g., on socialism, and defined in terms of elites who engage in power abuse, on the one hand, and citizens as victims, on the other hand, and hence *not populist but socialist*. On the right such an opposition is populist while it is used to manipulate the voters with social arguments not based on a corresponding social ideology. Since the identification of political parties should be formulated in terms of ideologies and/or positions of the Left-Right scale, and not in terms of strategic discourse structures, it does not make sense to speak of 'populist' parties in the first place. This implies that unless specific discourse structures are studied, it hardly makes sense to use 'populism' or 'populist' in the first place, as is the case in most studies of populism.

Hence, populism of the radical right is a *discursive* strategy with the following main characteristics (i) polarization between the People and the Elites, but understood as the defence Our Own People as a legitimation move, and Those in Power as political opponents, respectively; (ii) defence of (illiberal) attitudes that may get more votes in the country; (iii) a radical and provocative discourse style of ideological polarization (Us vs. Them), hyperboles, unfounded accusations, insults, offensive lexicon, and metaphors.

4.4 Ideologies and Attitudes of the Radical Right

The ideas of the radical right are not characterized by one, overall identifying ideology, defining an ideological group (as would be the case of socialists or feminists), but by *attitudes based on combinations of various ideologies,* such as racism (including, xenophobia, antisemitism, islamophobia, ethnic chauvinism), nationalism (including revisionism), sexism (including anti-feminism), Christianity (or Catholicism) and their norms (e.g., authority, respect, Law and Order), values (e.g., inequality), and ideological polarization (Us vs. Them).

4.5 The Attitudes and the Ideological Clusters of RR-parties Depend on the Economic, Cultural, Political, and Historical Contexts

All electoral programmes and their ideologies adapt to the *economic context* of the country. Especially in the Global South and the South of Europe, with widespread poverty, electoral programmes, also of RR parties, prominently focus on social policies for 'ordinary people'. Of course, these policies are limited to 'our' (white) people, and not immigrants or minorities, and more persuasively programmatic than in real policies where RR parties are in power. This is no less the case in the richer countries of the North, such as Sweden and the Netherlands, where socially vulnerable groups may be easily manipulated to vote for RR parties pretending to care for 'ordinary people'.

Similarly, in each country the radical right adapts its ideological position to the *sociocultural context* of the country. Thus, in culturally 'progressive' countries such as the Netherlands and Sweden, policies and attitudes against abortion or feminism and in favour of traditional family values would hardly increase votes and hence power, given the prevalent consensus on such attitudes, different from the radical right in such Catholic countries such as Spain or Chile. On the other hand, racist attitudes, especially anti-immigration, characterize the radical right (and more generally) all white-dominated countries, especially of the Global North.

This does not mean that nativist ideological clusters are absent in the Global South, where European ethnic groups are dominant. This is the case in Chile, where prejudice against Mapuche and recent immigrants from Venezuela are widespread but remain implicit in the electoral programme of the Radical Right, as shown in the total absence of references to the autochthonous Mapuche minority and its territorial and sociocultural claims. This is also one of the reasons why the progressive new constitution in Chile, proposed by the Left, was voted down: especially for the historically strong Radical Right, associated with the regime of Pinochet, it gave too much rights to the Mapuche.

Radical Right parties not only adapt their electoral programmes and their policies to the dominant cultural context of a country, but also to the *political context*. Thus, to compete with the Left, they claim to defend 'ordinary people' with social programmes, and within a discursive populist strategy associate the parties in power, especially those at the left, with a negative (e.g., corrupt) elite, as is especially explicit in the electoral programme of Vox in Spain. Within a nationalist ideology, the same programme also shows that major arguments of the Radical Right are especially persuasive in a political context of regional independence claims (as is the case for Catalonia) defined as a threat to a central, unified Nation. On the other hand, in Chile electoral support in the regions requires a programme and policy of decentralization, and an authoritarian reaction in a political context of student protest movement associated with the Left.

Finally, within the framework of nativist ideological clusters, also the *historical context* is relevant for countries with a colonial past, such as Spain and the Netherlands, whose RR parties typically defend revisionist attitudes about the glorious past of the country, civilizational supremacy, and the denial of colonial oppression. In the contemporary political context in Spain, such revisionism especially pertains to silencing the oppression of the dictatorial Franco regime, generally associated with the history of conservative parties, and the radical opposition against policies of 'Democratic Memory' about the Franco regime, typically associated with the Left.

References

Abdeslam, A. (2021). Muslims and immigrants in the populist discourse of the French party Rassemblement National and its leader on Twitter. Journal of Muslim Minority Affairs, 41(1), 46–61.

Agustin, O. (2019). Building left-wing populism in Denmark moving far away from the right. In Zienkowski, J., & Breeze, R., (Ed.), Imagining the peoples of Europe: Populist discourses across the political spectrum. (Vol. 83, pp. 149–171). Amsterdam Philadelphia: John Benjamins Publishing Company.

Akkerman, T., & Rooduijn, M. (2015). Pariahs or partners? Inclusion and exclusion of radical right parties and the effects on their policy positions. Political Studies, 63(5), 1140–1157.

Angouri, J., & Wodak, R. (2014). 'They became big in the shadow of the crisis': The Greek success story and the rise of the far right. Discourse & Society, 25(4), 540–565.

Arroyo Menéndez, M. (2020). Las causas del apoyo electoral a VOX en España. Política y Sociedad, 57(3), 693–717.

Askola, H. (2019). Wind from the North, don't go forth? Gender equality and the rise of populist nationalism in Finland. European Journal of Womens Studies, 26(1), 54–69.

Aslanidis, P. (2016). Is populism an ideology? A refutation and a new perspective. Political Studies, 64, 88–104.

Ballester Rodríguez, M. (2021). Vox y el uso de la historia: El relato del pasado remoto de España como instrumento político. Política y Sociedad, 58(2).

Ballester Rodríguez, M. (2023). Historia y guerra cultural en Vox. In Jesús María Casquete Badallo (Ed.), Vox frente a la historia. (pp. 15–24). Tres Cantos: Akal D.L.

Bar-On, T., & Molas, B. (Eds.). (2021). The right and radical right in the Americas: Ideological currents from interwar Canada to contemporary Chile. Lanham, MD: Lexington Books.

Barria Asenjo, N. A., Aguilera Hunt, R., Cabrera Sánchez, J., Letelier Soto, A., & Pinochet Mendoza, N. A. (2022). Ascenso de los discursos de extrema derecha en Chile: una aproximación desde la teoría crítica. Guillermo de Ockham: Revista científica, 20(2), 315–331.

Barrio, A., De Oger, S., & Field, B. (2021). Vox Spain: The organisational challenges of a new radical right Party. Politics and Governance, 9(4), 240–251.

Barrio, T. (2021). Populism in the 2019 general elections. Analysis of the speeches by the three right-wing candidates on Twitter. Communication & Society-Spain, 34(1), 123–141.

Bastow, S. (2019). The discourse of 19th-century French liberal socialism. Journal of Political Ideologies, 24(1), 93–112.

Bell, A. (1984). Language style as audience design. Language in Society, 13(2), 145–204.

Bernhard, L., & Kriesi, H. (2019). Populism in election times: A comparative analysis of 11 countries in Western Europe. West European Politics, 42(6), 1188–1208.

Björktomta, S. B. (2019). Honor-based violence in Sweden–Norms of honor and chastity. Journal of Family Violence, 34(5), 449–460.

Block, E. (2022). Disruptive discourse, populist communication and democracy: The cases of Hugo Chávez and Donald J. Trump. New York: Routledge.

Blofield, M. (2006). The politics of moral sin: Abortion and divorce in Spain, Chile and Argentina. New York: Routledge.

Boatright, R. G. (Ed.). (2019). A crisis of civility? Political discourse and its discontents. New York: Routledge.

Bobba, G., & McDonnell, D. (2016). Different types of right-wing populist discourse in government and opposition: The case of Italy. South European Society and Politics, 21(3), 281–299.

Bolin, N., Liden, G., & Nyhlen, J. (2014). Do anti-immigration parties matter? The case of the Sweden Democrats and local refugee policy. Scandinavian Political Studies, 37(3), 323–343.

Bonikowski, B. (2017). Ethno-nationalist populism and the mobilization of collective resentment. British Journal of Sociology, 68, 181–213.

Bonikowski, B., & Gidron, N. (2019). Populism in Legislative Discourse: Evidence from the European Parliament, 1999–2004. Working Paper.

Borges, A. (2021). Authoritarian inheritance, political conflict and conservative party institutionalisation: The cases of Chile and Brazil. Journal of Latin American Studies, 53(4), 767–793.

Braouezec, K. (2016). Identifying common patterns of discourse and strategy among the new extremist movements in Europe: The case of the English defence league and the bloc identitaire. Journal of Intercultural Studies, 37(6), 637–648.

Budge, I. (2015). Political parties: Manifestoes. In James D. Wright (Ed.), International encyclopedia of the social & behavioral sciences. (pp. 417–420). Amsterdam: Elsevier.

Budge, I., Robertson, David, & Hearl, D. (Eds.). (1987). Ideology, strategy, and party change: spatial analyses of post-war election programmes in 19 democracies. Cambridge: Cambridge University Press.

Bull, P., & Simon-Vandenbergen, A. (2014). Equivocation and doublespeak in far right-wing discourse: An analysis of Nick Griffin's performance on BBC's Question Time. Text & Talk, 34(1), 1–22.

Burke, S., Diba, P., & Antonopoulos, G. (2020). 'You sick, twisted messes': The use of argument and reasoning in Islamophobic and anti-Semitic discussions on Facebook. Discourse & Society, 31(4), 374–389.

Cagé, J., & Piketty, T. (2023). Une histoire du conflit politique. Élections et inégalités sociales en France, 1989–2022. Paris: Seuil.

Caiani, M., & Della Porta, D. (2011). The elitist populism of the extreme right: A frame analysis of extreme right-wing discourses in Italy and Germany. Acta Politica, 46(2), 180–202.

Camargo Fernández, L. (2021). El nuevo orden discursivo de la extrema derecha española: De la deshumanización a los bulos en un corpus de tuits de Vox sobre la inmigración. Cultura, Lenguaje y Representación = Culture, Language and Representation: Revista de Estudios Culturales de La Universitat Jaume I = Cultural Studies Journal of Universitat Jaume I, 26, 63–82.

Cammaerts, B. (2022). The abnormalisation of social justice: The 'anti-woke culture war' discourse in the Uk. Discourse & Society, 33(6), 730–743.

Cap, P., & Okulska, U. (Eds.). (2013). Analyzing genres in political communication. Theory and practice. Amsterdam: John Benjamins.

Cárdenas-Neira, C., & Pérez-Arredondo, C. (2021). Polarization and the educational conflict: A linguistic and multimodal approach to the discursive (re)construction of the Chilean student movement in the mainstream media and Facebook. In E. Morales López, L. Filardo Llamas, & A. Floyd (Eds.), Discursive approaches to socio-political polarization and conflict (pp. 174–191). London: Routledge.

Caro, I., & Quitral Rojas, M. (2023). La nueva derecha radical chilena en el contexto internacional: auge e ideología. Política y sociedad, 60(1), 1–16.

Castro Martínez, P., & Mo Groba, D. (2020). El issue de la inmigración en los votantes de VOX en las Elecciones Generales de noviembre de 2019. RIPS: Revista de Investigaciones Políticas y Sociológicas, 19(1), 39–58.

Cervi, L., Tejedor, S., & Villar, M. (2023). Twitting against the enemy: Populist radical right parties discourse against the (political) 'other'. Politics and Governance, 11(2), 235–248.

Charalambous, G., & Ioannou, G. (Eds.). (2019). Left radicalism and populism in Europe. London: Routledge.

Darian-Smith, E. (2023). Deadly global alliance: Antidemocracy and anti-environmentalism. Third World Quarterly, 44(2), 284–299.

De Lange, S., & Mugge, L. (2015). Gender and right-wing populism in the low countries: Ideological variations across parties and time. Patterns of Prejudice, 49(1–2), 61–80.

Dekker, P., Boonstoppel, E., Hurenkamp, M., Middendorp, I., & Tonkens, E. (2020). Dealen met de grote wereld: Globalisering in de publieke opinie en op het werk. The Hague: Sociaal en Cultureel Planbureau.

Diaz, C., Kaltwasser, C., & Zanotti, L. (2023). The arrival of the populist radical right in Chile Jose Antonio Kast and the 'Partido Republicano'. Journal of Language and Politics, 22(3), 342–359.

Dietze, G., & Roth, J. (Eds.). (2020). Right-wing populism and gender: European perspectives and beyond. Bielefeld: Transcript.

Eckert, P., & Rickford, J. R. (Eds.). (2001). Style and sociolinguistic variation. Cambridge: Cambridge University Press.

Edwards, G. (2012). A comparative discourse analysis of the construction of 'in-groups' in the 2005 and 2010 manifestos of the British National Party. Discourse & Society, 23(3), 245–258.

Ekman, M., & Krzyzanowski, M. (2021). A populist turn? News editorials and the recent discursive shift on immigration in Sweden. Nordicom Review, 42, 67–87.

Ekström, M., Patrona, M., & Thornborrow, J. (2018). Right-wing populism and the dynamics of style: A discourse-analytic perspective on mediated political performances. Palgrave Communications, 4(1), 1–11.

Elgenius, G., & Rydgren, J. (2017). The Sweden Democrats and the ethno-nationalist rhetoric of decay and betrayal. Sociologisk Forskning, 54(4), 353–358.

Elgenius, G., & Rydgren, J. (2019). Frames of nostalgia and belonging: The resurgence of ethno-nationalism in Sweden. European Societies, 21(4), 583–602.

Engstrom, R., & Paradis, C. (2015). The in-group and out-groups of the British National Party and the UK Independence Party a corpus-based discourse-historical analysis. Journal of Language and Politics, 14(4), 501–527.

Farre, J. (2017). The rhetoric of the extreme in the Chilean far right. Hallazgos-Revista de Invesitigaciones, 14(27), 19–41.

Feldman, O. (Ed.). (2023). Debasing political rhetoric: Dissing opponents, journalists, and minorities in populist leadership communication. Cham: Springer.

Feldman, M., & Jackson, P. (Eds.). (2014). Doublespeak: The rhetoric of the radical right since 1945. Stuttgart: Ibidem-Verlag.

Fernández Riquelme, P. (2020). Identidad y nostalgia: El discurso de vox a través de tres eslóganes. SABIR: International Bulletin Of Applied Linguistics, 1(2), 77–114.

Fernández Sánchez, G. (2019). España: VOX, ¿arcaísmo o modernidad? In F. Delle Donne & A. Jerez (Eds.), Epidemia ultra: La ola reaccionaria que contagia a Europa (pp. 95–109). Berlín?: Andreu Jerez.

Ferreira, C. (2019). Vox como representante de la derecha radical en España: Un estudio sobre su ideología. Revista Española de Ciencia Política, 51, 73–98.

Flesher Fominaya, C. (2020). Democracy reloaded: Inside Spain's political laboratory from 15-M to Podemos. New York: Oxford University Press.

Forchtner, B. (Ed.). (2020). The radical right and the environment: Politics, discourse and communication. London: Routledge.

Forchtner, B., & Ozvatan, O. (2022). De/legitimising Europe through the performance of crises the far-right alternative for Germany on 'climate hysteria' and 'corona hysteria'. Journal of Language and Politics, 21(2), 208–232.

Garrido Rubia, A., & Mora, A. (2020). Populismo y extrema derecha: El discurso de VOX. In E. Jaráiz, Gulías, A. Cazorla Martín, & M. Pereira López (Eds.), El auge de la extrema derecha en España (pp. 349–382). Valencia?: Tirant lo Blanch.

González Fuentes, J. A. (2017). La retórica de lo extremo en la ultraderecha chilena. Hallazgos, revista de investigaciones, 14(27), 19–41.

Harrison, S., & Bruter, M. (2011). Mapping extreme right ideology: An empirical geography of the European extreme right. Houndmills, Basingstoke: Palgrave Macmillan.

Hidalgo Tenorio, E., Benitez-Castro, M. A., & De Cesare, F. (Eds.). (2019). Populist discourse: Critical approaches to contemporary politics. London: Routledge.

Hilhorst, S., & Hermes, J. (2016). 'We have given up so much': Passion and denial in the Dutch Zwarte Piet (Black Pete) controversy. European Journal of Cultural Studies, 19(3), 218–233.

Hutton, C. (2017). Racial ideology as elite discourse: Nordicism and the visual in an age of mass culture. Social Semiotics, 27(3), 335–347.

Jagers, J., & Walgrave, S. (2007). Populism as political communication style: An empirical study of political parties' discourse in Belgium. European Journal of Political Research, 46(3), 319–345.

Keil, A. (2020). 'We need to rediscover our manliness . . .' the language of gender and authenticity in German right-wing populism. Journal of Language and Politics, 19(1), 107–124.

Kelsey, D. (2016). Hero mythology and right-wing populism: A discourse-mythological case study of Nigel Farage in the mail online. Journalism Studies, 17(8), 971–988.

Kopytowska, M. W. (Ed.). (2017). Contemporary discourses of hate and radicalism across space and genres. Amsterdam: John Benjamins.

Koller, V. et al. (2023). Voices of supporters: Populism, social media and the 2019 European elections (Discourse approaches to politics, society and culture 101). Amsterdam: Benjamins.

Kottig, M. (2016). Gender and radical right politics in Europe. New York: Macmillan.

Kumarasingham, H. (Ed.). (2020). Liberal ideals and the politics of decolonisation. Routledge.

Laclau, E. (2005). On populist reason. London: Verso.

Lamour, C. (2022). Orban Urbi et Orbi: Christianity as a nodal point of radical-right populism. Politics and Religion, 15(2), 317–343.

Laube, S. (2020). The adapted position: Preparing political contents for a hybrid media environment. Media Culture & Society, 42(2), 155–171.

Leezenberg, M. (2015). Discursive violence and responsibility: Notes on the pragmatics of Dutch populism. Journal of Language Aggression and Conflict, 3(1), 200–228.

Lemmens, K. (2017). The dark side of 'Zwarte Piet': A misunderstood tradition or racism in disguise? A legal analysis. International Journal of Human Rights, 21(2), 120–141.

Macaulay, M. (Ed.). (2019). Populist discourse: International perspectives. Cham: Springer.

March, L. (2017). Left and right populism compared: The British case. British Journal of Politics & International Relations, 19(2), 282–303.

Mudde, C. (2000). Ideology of the extreme right. Manchester: Manchester University Press.

Mudde, C. (2010). The Populist radical right: A pathological normalcy. West European Politics, 33(6), 1167–1186.

Mudde, C. (2014). Fighting the system? Populist radical right parties and party system change. Party Politics, 20(2), 217–226.

Mudde, C. (2019). The radical right today. London: Routledge.

Mudde, C. (Ed.). (2017). The populist radical right: A reader. London: Routledge.

Mudde, C., & Rovira Kaltwasser, C. (2017). Populism: A very short introduction. Oxford: Oxford University Press.

Mudde, C., & Rovira Kaltwasser, C. (2018): Studying populism in comparative perspective: Reflections on the contemporary and future research agenda. Comparative Political Studies, 51(13), 1667–1693.

Muis, J., & Immerzeel, T. (2017). Causes and consequences of the rise of populist radical right parties and movements in Europe. Current Sociology, 65(6), 909–930.

Musolff, A. (2022). Fake conspiracy: Trump's anti-Chinese 'COVID-19-as-war' scenario. In M. Demata, V. Zorzi, & A. Zottola. (Eds.), Conspiracy theory discourses. (pp. 121–139). Amsterdam: Benjamins.

Norris, P., & Inglehart, R. (2018). Cultural backlash: Trump, Brexit, and the rise of authoritarian-populism. New York: Cambridge University Press.

Olmeda Gómez, J. A. (2020). VOX. Entre el liberalismo conservador y la derecha identitaria. Revista Española de Ciencia Política, 54, 175–182.

Oztig, L. (2023). Islamophobic discourse of European right-wing parties: A narrative policy analysis. Social Currents, 10(3), 225–244.

Palacios-Valladares, I. (2020). Chile's 2019 October protests and the student movement: Eventful mobilization? Revista de Ciencia Politica, 40(2), 215–234.

Pallarés-Navarro, S., & Zugasti, R. (2022). Santiago Abascal's Twitter and Instagram strategy in the 10 November 2019 General Election Campaign: A populist approach to discourse and leadership? Communication & Society, 35(2), 53–69.

Pascale, C. (2019). The weaponization of language: Discourses of rising right-wing authoritarianism. Current Sociology, 67(6), 898–917.

Prothero, S. R. (2016). Why liberals win the culture wars (even when they lose elections): The battles that define America from Jefferson's heresies to gay marriage. New York: HarperOne, an imprint of HarperCollins.

Rama, J., Zanotti, L., Turnbull-Dugarte, S. J., & Santana, A. (2021). VOX: The rise of the Spanish populist radical right. London: Routledge.

Ravndal, J. (2018). Right-wing terrorism and militancy in the Nordic countries: A comparative case study. Terrorism and political violence, 30(5), 772–792.

Rheindorf, M., & Wodak, R. (Eds.). (2019). Sociolinguistic perspectives on migration control: Language policy, identity and belonging. Blue Ridge Summit, PA: Multilingual Matters.

Rodenberg, J., & Wagenaar, P. (2016). Essentializing 'Black Pete': Competing narratives surrounding the Sinterklaas tradition in the Netherlands. International Journal of Heritage Studies, 22(9), 716–728.

Rooduijn, M. (2014a). The nucleus of populism: In search of the lowest common denominator. Government and Opposition, 49(4), 572–598.

Rooduijn, M. (2014b). Vox populismus: A populist radical right attitude among the public? Nations and Nationalism, 20(1), 80–92.

Rooduijn, M. (2019). State of the field: How to study populism and adjacent topics? A plea for both more and less focus. European Journal of Political Research, 58, 362–372.

Rooduijn, M., & Akkerman, T. (2017). Flank attacks: Populism and left-right radicalism in Western Europe. Party Politics, 23(3), 193–204.

Rooduijn, M., Bonikowski, B., & Parlevliet, J. (2021). Populist and nativist attitudes: Does ingroup/outgroup thinking spill over across domains? European Union Politics, 22(2), 248–265.

Rooduijn, M., & Van Kessel, S. (2019). Populism and Euroskepticism in the European Union. In F. Laursen (Ed.), Oxford Encyclopedia of European Union Politics. Oxford University Press.

Rovira Kaltwasser, C., Taggart, P. A., Ochoa Espejo, P., & Ostiguy, P. (2017). The Oxford handbook of populism. Oxford: Oxford University Press.

Rydgren, J. (2007). The sociology of the radical right. Annual Review of Sociology, 33, 241–262.

Sanahuja Perales, J. A., & López Burian, C. (2022). Hispanidad e Iberosfera: Antiglobalismo, internacionalismo reaccionario y ultraderecha neopatriota en Iberoamérica. Documentos de trabajo (Fundación Carolina): Segunda época, 69.

Schumacher, G., Rooduijn, M., & Bakker, B. (2022). Hot populism? affective responses to antiestablishment rhetoric. Political Psychology, 43(5), 851–871.

Serafis, D., & Boukala, S. (2023). Subtle hate speech and the recontextualisation of antisemitism online: Analysing argumentation on Facebook. In Esposito, E., & KhosraviNik, M. (Eds.), Discourse in the digital age (pp. 143–167). London: Routledge.

Sniderman, P. M., Petersen, M. B., Slothuus, R., & Stubager, R. (2014). Paradoxes of liberal democracy: Islam, Western Europe, and the Danish cartoon crisis. Princeton, NJ: Princeton University Press.

Solomos, J. (Ed.). (2020). Routledge international handbook of contemporary racisms. Abingdon: Routledge.

Stavrakakis, Y., Katsambekis, G., Nikisianis, N., Kioupkiolis, A., & Siomos, T. (2017). Extreme right-wing populism in Europe: Revisiting a reified association. Critical Discourse Studies, 14(4), 420–439.

Steger, M. (2019). Mapping antiglobalist populism bringing ideology back in. Populism, 2(2), 110–136.

Suarez, B. (2021). Gender and immigration in vox: The discourse of the radical right in Spain. Migraciones, 51, 241–268.

Sznajder, M. (2015). Politics in History: The Chilean radical right in the 20th century. Araucaria-Revista Iberoamericana de Filosoifia Politica y Humanidades, 17(34), 177–201.

Valencia-García, L. D. (Ed.). (2020). Radical-Right revisionism and the end of history. Alt / histories. New York: Routledge/Taylor & Francis Group.

Van Dijk, T. A. (1984). Prejudice in discourse: An analysis of ethnic prejudice in cognition and conversation. Amsterdam: J. Benjamins Pub. Co.

Van Dijk, T. A. (1988). Sinterklaas en Zwarte Piet: Is het racism of is 't het niet? In L. Helder & S. Gravenberch (Eds.), Sinterklaasje, kom maar binnen met je knecht, (pp: 118–135). Berchem: Epo.

Van Dijk, T. A. (1991). Racism and the Press. London: Routledge.

Van Dijk, T. A. (1992). Discourse and the denial of racism. Discourse & Society, 3(1), 87–118.

Van Dijk, T. A. (1993). Elite discourse and racism. Newbury Park, CA: Sage Publications.

Van Dijk, T. A. (1998). Ideology: A multidisciplinary approach. London: Sage Publications.

Van Dijk, T. A. (2003). De Rasoel-Komrij affaire. Amsterdam: Critics.

Van Dijk, T. A. (2008). Discourse and context: A sociocognitive approach. Cambridge: Cambridge University Press.

Van Dijk, T. A. (2014). Discourse and knowledge: A sociocognitive approach. New York: Cambridge University Press.

Van Dijk, T. A. (2021a). Antiracist discourse: Theory and history of a macro-movement. Cambridge: Cambridge University Press.

Van Dijk, T. A. (2021b). Are ideologies negative? Published in I. Fairclough, J. Mulderrig & K. Zotzmann (Eds.), Language and power: Essays in honour of Norman Fairclough (pp. 147–155). Amazon, Independent Publication.

Van Dijk, T. A. (2023a) Analyzing frame analysis. Discourse Studies, 25(2), 153–178.

Van Dijk, T. A. (2023b). Social movement discourse: Manifestos. In C. R. Caldas-Coulthard and M. Coulthard (Eds.), Texts and practices: Readings in critical discourse analysis. 2nd Edn (pp. 113–133). London: Routledge.

Van Dijk, T. A. (2023c). Social movement discourse: An introduction. London: Routledge.

Van Dijk, T. A. (2023d). Interview Teun A. van Dijk on Populism, Ideology, Discursive Strategies, and the Reactionary Right. Illiberalism.org.

Van Prooijen, J.-W. (2019). Overconfidence in radical politics. In: J. P. Forgas, W.D. Crano & K. Fiedler (Eds.), The psychology of populism: The tribal challenge to liberal democracy. (pp. 143–157). London: Routledge.

Venegas, M. (2021). Against women: The misogynist discourse of Vox. 'Growling words' of Spanish national-populism. Investigaciones Feministas, 12(1), 67–77.

Verkuyten, M., & Nooitgedagt, W. (2019). Parliamentary identity and the management of the radical right: A discursive analysis of Dutch parliamentary debates. British Journal of Social Psychology, 58(3), 495–514.

Vossen, K. (2017). The power of populism: Geert Wilders and the party for freedom in the Netherlands. London: Routledge and Taylor & Francis Group.

Weyland, K. (1996) 'Neopopulism and neoliberalism in Latin America: Unexpected affinities', Studies in Comparative International Development, 31(3), 3–31.

Wodak, R. (2009). The discursive construction of national identity. Edinburgh: Edinburgh University Press.

Wodak, R. (2021). The politics of fear: The shameless normalization of radical right discourse. 2nd ed. London: Sage.

Wodak, R., KhosraviNik, M., & Mral, B. (Eds.) (2013). Right wing populism in Europe: Politics and discourse. London: Bloomsbury Academic.

Wuthnow, R. (1989) Communities of discourse: Ideology and social structure in the reformation, the enlightenment, and European socialism. Cambridge, MA: Harvard University Press.

Zienkowski, J., & Breeze, R. (Eds.) (2019). Imagining the peoples of Europe. Populist discourses across the political spectrum. Amsterdam Philadelphia: John Benjamins Publishing Company.

About the Author

Teun A. van Dijk (1943) was Professor of Discourse Studies at the University of Amsterdam until his retirement in 2004, and since 1999 Professor of Discourse Studies at Pompeu Fabra University, Barcelona. Since 2017 he is founding director of the Centre of Discourse Studies, Barcelona (www.discoursestudies.org). After his earlier work on generative poetics, text grammar, and the psychology of discourse processing, his work since the 1980s takes a more critical turn, and focuses on the relations between discourse and (anti)racism, news, power, ideology, context, and knowledge, areas in which he published several books and articles. His recent work is on social movement discourse and the radical right. He was founding Editor of the international journals *Poetics* and *Text* (now *Text & Talk*), and the online journal *Discurso & Sociedad* (www.dissoc.org) and is currently founding Editor of *Discourse & Society, Discourse Studies, Discourse & Communication*. Teun A. van Dijk holds three honorary doctorates and has extensively lectured worldwide, especially in Latin America, where he founded, in 1995, with Adriana Bolivar, the Latinamerican Association of Discourse Studies (ALED). For detail on his publications, see his website www.discourses.org. E-mail: vandijk@discourses.org.

Cambridge Elements ☰

Critical Discourse Studies

Gavin Brookes
Lancaster University

Gavin Brookes is Research Fellow and UKRI Future Leader Fellow in the Department of Linguistics and English Language at Lancaster University (UK). His research utilises techniques and approaches from Critical Discourse Studies, Corpus Linguistics and Multimodal Discourse Studies in order to investigate the connection between discourse and social life, particularly in health(care), institutional and media contexts. As well as being series co-editor for Cambridge Elements in Critical Discourse Studies, Gavin sits on the editorial boards of a number of journals and is Associate Editor of the International Journal of Corpus Linguistics (John Benjamins) and Co-Editor of the Corpus and Discourse book series (Bloomsbury).

Veronika Koller
Lancaster University

Veronika Koller is Professor of Discourse Studies in the Department of Linguistics and English Language at Lancaster University (UK). Her research centres on Critical Discourse Studies, employing corpus linguistic, systemic functional linguistics and other approaches to investigate political discourse, business communication and discourses on language, gender and sexuality. She has a special interest in the form and function of metaphor in discourse. Veronika is an editorial board member for various international journals and Associate Editor for the journal Metaphor and Symbol. Next to her academic career, she has experience as a consultant and corporate speaker.

About the Series

The Elements series presents work on theoretical and methodological advancements in critical discourse studies (CDS), along with reports on original research which has been carried out from a linguistic perspective. Individual works cluster around topics such as identities in political discourse, (social) media discourses or language, discrimination and conflict. Within these and other topics, we particularly welcome contributions which develop subject areas, e.g. looking at the discourse 'by' rather than 'on' migrants, or investigating societal conflict in discourses around climate change.

Cambridge Elements $\equiv$

Critical Discourse Studies

Elements in the Series

Discourse and Ideologies of the Radical Right
Teun A. van Dijk

A full series listing is available at: www.cambridge.org/ECDS